.

IJYNX

by

BLAIR MacKENZIE BLAKE

First privately published by the author in a limited edition of 200 numbered and signed copies, with a revised second edition of 600 copies published to coincide with the Autumnal Equinox, 2004 e.v. The current edition published in 2008 of the common era in order to remind each sentient entity of the entelechy of the dead.

Cover Design by:
Camella Grace and Adam Jones
Edits for new edition by Mark James Foster and Greg Taylor

ISBN: 978-0-9757200-3-5
This edition published by Daily Grail Publishing in 2008

CONTENTS

Sun's Black Majesty	13
Uroboros	15
Mummia (Seraphim of Thanatos)	17
Xepera	19
1. Bloodstains on Embroidery	
2. Xeperu	
3. Of Weavings Encrimsoned	
Grimorium de Argentum Virgium	23
Stellar Wisdom	25
In Ancient Moonlight: The Glimmerings of Luciftia, an Atlantean Brain	33
Spectrophilia	41
Netjeryt	43
Silvered Leaves of Goetic Prayers (from the Sirian Goetia)	51
Xibalba (Starfire Blood-Feasts)	53
Parsons Krater	59
Egyptian Blue Sunshine	61
The Jewel of Divine Anthropophagy	63
A Cornucopiae Between Compasses	65
Enhaloing the Lamanaut	67
Of the Unearthing of the Stolen Brilliance of Zu	71
Magistelli	81
Eroto-Comatose Lucidity	85
Da'ath of Babalon	87
Blue Lipstick	91
Lachrymatory	93
Reliquary	95
1. Beauseant	
2. Mfkzt	
3. Ijynx	
4. Tailleoir	
The Black Wine of Owls	99
Ophiuchus	101
Calix Horroris	103

I am the flame that burns in every heart of man,
and in the core of every star. I am Life,
and the giver of Life, yet therefore is the
knowledge of me the knowledge of death.

LIBER AL
vel LEGIS
CAP. 2, V. 6

Write, & find ecstasy in writing!

LIBER AL
vel LEGIS
CAP. 2, V. 66

IJYNX

the grand dreaming of a treasured eye

FOREWORD

Writing in his book, *Atlantis: The Lost Continent (Liber LI)*, the renowned British occultist, Aleister Crowley, states that "the word for Magic, ijynx, was the only dissyllable in the language, for Magic was the essentially two-fold thing, more two-fold (in a way) than the number two itself." Although most students of western esotericism have concluded that Crowley's *Liber LI* is a further example of allegorical 'high-jinks' veiling a treatise of left-hand path sex-magick (no doubt due to cryptic phrases in the preface such as "dreaming true" and "preparation of the antinomy"), it is the present author's belief that the book actually both conceals and reveals a higher Arcanum involving a highly-specialized form of esoteric cannibalism practiced by a necrophagous cult older than the earliest dynasties of ancient Egypt (Khem).

Bearing this in mind, rather than being the submerged land-mass of an advanced maritime civilization (much less a spacefaring civilization with super-sophisticated technology), the mythological lost continent in Plato's dialogue in *Timaeus* symbolizes a hidden (lost?) dimension or realm of consciousness - an otherworldly kaleidoscope populated by a consortium of hyper-dimensional intelligences, and, furthermore, the valuable orichalcum dug out of the 'earth' by the Atlanteans was in reality a mysterious post-mortem endogenous substance known variously as "Occultum of Harlequin", "The Residuum of Paradise", "The Glitter of the Sleepers" and "The Dream of the Dreamless." In a rather ingenious cryptogram, Crowley comes close to revealing the exact nature of this death-born residue when, in speaking about the 'houses' of Atlas (Atlas being the king from which Atlantis received its name), he informs us that "the pavements were rough and broken almost everywhere" for a reason which he (Crowley) was not permitted to disclose. With some curious etymology, he offers another hint by telling us that the root for the name Atlas is the Lemurian 'Tla' or 'Tlas' meaning black.

Blair MacKenzie Blake
December 1st, 2003 e.v.

FOREWORD TO THE CURRENT EDITION

A reader of the foreword to the second edition of this book has claimed that it is a further example of *obscurum per obscurious*, a phrase used by certain grudging alchemists in describing their own writings, meaning to explain the obscure by the more obscure. In the spirit of "that black which makes black white", to this I will only add: In Chapter Three of Aleister Crowley's *Liber LI*, the author states that, according to the most ancient tradition of the Atlantean magicians, they were the survivors of the sunken continent of Lemuria, whose inhabitants, through a misunderstanding of the 23rd magical law (some said the 2nd, some the 8th), "had involved themselves and their land in ruin. [But] others thought that the Lemurians had succeeded in their magical task and [had] broken their temple." Using the X marks the spot on this treasure map of sorts, hopefully aided with certain Crowleyan techniques to enhance concentration and overcome any breaks, it is possible to, once again, locate (if not extract) the Jewel of Divine Anthropophagy...but only by keeping in mind (again, quoting from Crowley's *Liber LI*) "the prime axiom of the Atlanteans of attaining things through their opposites."

Blair MacKenzie Blake
October 12th, 2007 e.v.

Sun's Black Majesty

Green falcon alighting upon the heart of the aurora,
Slayer of the fleece of the iridescent lamb with seven eyes.
Eighth chakra* opened in the trance of beatitude,
Spectrum of illusions dissolved in the garden of mystery.
Prince drinking the colors of Isis in the desert of engilded night.
Bedecked in the purple robe of mystical kingship.
Sacred island of jewels reached with Luzifer's recovered wings,
Silver plumage of swan gliding across the starry drapery.
Midnight angels trumpeting at the palace of gleaming pillars,
Fields of Arcadia blossoming in the treasure of black fire.
Aurific seed hidden in the womb of eternity,
Beyond the prism of light in the portal of the snake-nebula.
Lotus-flower of Da'ath† in waters of harlequin fish,
Facets of the crown adorning the daughter of the violet star.
Ray of esoteric luminary shining upon the king of radiant blood,
Enthroned in etheric blue with a nimbus of immortality.

---

* Originally, the word I chose to use here contained the ancient Sanskrit root-word arka, which according to one modern etymologicon is related to a particular ray or flash, and from which the Latin word for silver, *argentum*, is derived. However, when combined with 'ch' the result has proven to be both dangerous and illegal, magickally speaking. Therefore, for this edition, I have changed it to the more common "decorative convention," a word also associated with a specific vortex of energy as well as a certain 'jeweled' vector that remains quite secretive.

† Here I am not speaking of the blue water lily (*Nymphaea caerulea*) depicted in magical papyri and funerary stelae of the dynastic Egyptians, although at some stage psychotropic flora may have been used by the priesthood of Heliopolis as a substitute for the true "Residuum of Paradise" as a vehicle of shamanic ecstasies.

Uroboros

Violet eyes shine.
Jeweled water of the living graal,
Gilded, stainless vessel 'neath the prismatic lamp of Abraxas.
Night-blue draperies a-glitter with cosmic opulence,
Tides of blood aurified in her sacred chalice.
Radiant white-plumed dove shedding tears of rainbow wine,
Mooncup of red-gold with swirls of oily iridescence.
Lady of the serpent holding a richly-crowned babe,
Nurtured with gemmed drops of the milk of paradise.
Face enhaloed with light adored by amethyst-lidded eyes,
Child of great serenity protected by majestic wings,
Perfumed gauze of the vesture of the dragon-queen.
Spooned from calyx horroris the rich food of the matrix,
Extracts of the perfect ruby flowing from her hidden spring.
Bestowing mystic sight to the prince in wisps of azure garment,
A wondrous flowering upon the deathless green.

Slain lamb bleeding the rarest colors,
Royal secret in morsels of dainty meats.
In those rosy fingers, a golden wafer held,
Sweet like the honey of breasts.

Majesty of a tawny lion in the aurora of a lustrous sun,
Anointed harlequin king enthroned in the Temple of Midnight.
Feast of crimson cakes offered by the peacock angel,
Horn of plenty from the purity of silver nectar.
Orange-gold galaxies in a Krater of celestial firefoam,
Tower of ivory bedecked with the exiled emerald stone
Held in purple gloves of ornate, pattern-draped kings
Swallowing heart-drops of the virgin's unfading glory.
Scarlet-jetted fountain of the unmated mother
Converted into a vehicle of the highest light.
Vivified dreams reached by mercurial swan-chariot,
Tapestry of paradise hidden in a flame's black majesty.
Shimmer of kingdoms in spring's gemmed rain,
Blessed greenness of the companions of the Sangraal,
Jeweled flesh of the living treasure.
Violet eyes shine.

Mummia

(Seraphim of Thanatos)

Painted sunset of a desolate valley,
Blood-red dunes of scorpion in the intruder's eye.
Birds at twilight o'er drifts of lavender sand
As shadows of camels pass unhindered on a deserted path.
Many-breasted fig crowned with pale sprinkling of stars,
Faces observing a signal fire on the approaching cliffs.
Vizier's secret plotting 'neath the drifting moon,
Bribing necropolis guards with brazen impudence.
Entering the tomb-caverns with burning torches,
Tongues of flame in the pupils of the jackal.

Nest of snakes hissing at the dust of sandals,
Halo of votive niches in the catacombs of dragon-kings.
Sepulchral lamps ablaze with magnificent oil,
Dim-gilded catafalque reflecting flickers of orange.
Flame-patterns on wings of burnished gold,
Cherubic beasts flourishing opaline swords.
Turquoise stele detailed from the scribe's palette,
Intricate reliefs of reed-dipped colors.
Vignettes on limestone lifted in the resplendent glow,
Violet eyes of true nobility staring at the gates of eternity.
Preserved splendor laid in an ornate sarcophagus,
Shrouded in gilt-purple befitting his majesty.
Solemnity of bitumen in the treasure room,
Sapphire over heart draped with musty, embroidered pomp.
Weapons of divine forging in folds of unfaded crimson,
Sunless eye of emerald scepter in the painted tomb.
Fire-thrilled diadem studded with precious stones,
Vivid glowing hues in the palace of gloom.

Golden spoils undisturbed by thievish hands,
Aureole of severed head placed in a sack of leather.
Kingly visage with the mark of exalted birth,
Babe suckled on the throne of the lily of purity,
Nurtured from rivulets of ivory-gilded breasts,
Prince receiving sustenance from starfire bloodfests.
Night-canopied brows smeared with virginal honey,
Prized eye bleeding 'neath lamps of star-clusters.
Riding the swan of ecstasy in the richness of light,
Enduring sinew in the glorious robe of promise.
Veins with immortal black blood of pyramidal lords
From sacred blue heart of gemmed navel cord.
Inheritors of the rainbow stone gnawed by death-worms,
Haunted by specters at dusk in a nimbus of mauve.
Effacing traces of footprints with a broom of palm leaves,
Nightly getaway to the sanctuary of the gnosis
To feast on glittering veins of pulverized bones
In a desert of silver whose thorns burst into flower.

Fleeing the aura of gold in the burial chamber
For jewels spilled across the desert skies.
Nostrils blackened with the taste of cadaverous perfumes,
Sangraal kings embalmed with the crocodile of the waters.
Password given with the crunch of footsteps,
Silvery darting of the moon in a camel's painted eye.
Grisly relic placed in saddle-bags,
Systematic plunder of the sacrament of death.
Occult gold to feed the light-body of the pharaoh,
Ingestible mummia of harlequin kings.

Xepera

(With purity cultivated from the germ,
Imperishable as this star–metall'd arthame,
Encircle with violet flame, thy region charged…)

Bloodstains on Embroidery

Plumes of dust spreading like crimson veils
Across an orange flaming disk sinking in the West.
Tails of shaggy beasts flicking the pastel horizon,
A lamp extinguished (of its azure flame)
Dulling the brass plaques of traveling-boxes.
Maiden's eyes like the emeralds of Nubia
Peering from the decorative tent of a caravan encamped.
Daughter of the painted Nile in finely-embroidered linen
Alarmed by the shrieks of a circling hawk.
Perfumes of silvery-green grapes,
Spicy scents mingled with the odor of camel sweat.
Skin of carnelian ornamented with protective amulets,
Heart pounding while clutching blossoms of garlic.
Filled with horror at droplets on a sequined litter-cushion,
Rich opaque cloth moistened with her ruby tears
When across the haunted stretches a flash of green
Like the malachite-stained eyelids of beauty,
Sleeper of the sands awakening at the fires of sunset.

Xeperu

Night unfurling like a glittering scroll
'Till palm fronds are etched against the vaulted splendor.
Prismatic lamps aglow in halls of arched sandstone,
Polychrome mosaic floor carpeted with the pelts of leopards.
Royal fan-bearers like polished ebony gemmed,
Gold pectorals amid the whisper of purple heron feathers.
Brilliant king ruling with elegant aplomb
Seated upon a throne of onyx and bdellium.
Harlequin tapestry of the palace hung with gilt-incense thuribles,
Body adornments of a torso twisting in the bluish swirls.
Veil dancing to a melodious bone,
Dropping scarves of violet mist to reveal slender nut-brown curves.
Sheer fluid fabric in a lion's amber eyes,
Musky glamour born at twilight with anise-flavored wine.
Flame patterns on the jangle of tarnished bangles
Tinged with colors like the Nile's burnished water.
Flourishing gestures of fingers with embellishing rings,
Undraping gauze fluttering like imaginary wings.
Glistening dark charms of a serpentine dance,
Moving languidly between gaily-painted papyrus columns.

Wisps of violet on a mosaic of glazed tiles
As opulent pylons flare in the hypostyle hall.
Noble brows diademed with law in the aureole of lamps,
Prince of the dragon blood in his profusely decorated lair.
Kneeling before the gossamer fragility of a beatific vision,
Beloved daughter in floating draperies of pale lilac.
Taste of honeycakes and figs on lips richly bedecked,
Plaited braids with perfumed unguents of bitter almond.
Skin of Egyptian copper tattooed with indigo tracery,
Amethyst-tinted lids adorned with reed.
Inviting the golden straw of the vampyre,
Night-winged for the ritual ceremony in a drape of vermilion.
Divine flux of the feeding maiden vivid to the nostrils,
Immortal riches in her nectar of deep garnet red.
Scarlet jets staining the opalescence of gilded nails,
Majesty of the dunes slaked with the jeweled water of dark paradise.
Shape-shifting like ripples of magenta in the gathering dusk,
Flecks of royal apparel upon the floor like brittle plaster.
Magic flesh dripping from the kingly figure
Assuming the shape of his reptoid ancestor.

Of Weavings Encrimsoned

Chariot of the dawning sun traversing the sapphire void
As beturbaned faces drink from tawny waterskins.
Fevered visions of a maiden astride a camel
Sprawled on damask in the glittering trace of cerulean.
Shape of terror against the nimbus of the orange door
Appearing as a solitary kite wheeling in the hazy afterglow.
Curtained lids restless with the shadows of crystal night-lamps,
Rustling wings of demons like the shrilling of papyrus beds.
Spectral flight of a dream over moon-ensilvered dunes,
Abducted from her tent to the scepter of authority.
Starry plains crowning an oasis of persea and tamarisk,
Variegated lights of an imposing desert fortress.
Nocturnal ecstasies in the halo of a purple lantern,
Sparkling facets of gems in the valley of richly-costumed breasts.
Sandals of leather among tinsel and glamour
Gone now like arabesques of spider-silk in a sudden gust.
Clutching a scarab against the pageantry of her heart
While bumped upon a pillow stained like mummy ocher.

Grimorium de Argentum Virgium

Writhing in ecstasy amid night's glittering beatitude,
Priestess of magical chastity recumbent on crimson damask.
Naked splendor enflamed like a palm against the starry tapestry,
Blissfully enlaced with a lover the dream enweaves.
Tactile ivory flesh limned with kalas of decorous fire
Tinging the veil of pearl-grey mist with glorious astral colors.
Spasms of pleasure at the point of climax,
Trumpeting raptures with ejaculations of gemmed light.
Eroticism of sleep in a mirror slanted to the interstellar deeps,
Matrimonial bed ornamented with voluptuous celestial joys.
Orbit of mystery eclipsed by the zodiac's fieriest talisman,
Ashen dove of the hidden rainbow above the seven palaces.
Rich sunset painting a camel crossing the lavender desert,
Images in supreme darkness revealed with the treasure of angelic eyes:
Jeweled apple ripening in the death of paradise,
Perfect fruit of the serpent in the aura of the maiden's silver.
Luxurious feast of the Mass of flaming sapphire,
Blood of the gilded lion mingled with the saliva of the pinkest rose.
Intricacies of red in cosmic veins of the crowned shining being,
Seed of the prismatic tree conceived from terrestrial facets.
Virginal Womb enhaloed with the Avatar of the Eleventh Hour,
Majesty of the starchild with the shyness of violet eyes.
Aura of enthroned king in soft, golden metallic swathings,
Ecstasy's vision breathing the luminous serenity.

Stellar Wisdom

Vibrations
startling the reptilian pose basking in dappled golden warmth
When a kaleidoscopic blaze in the umbrage of laced fernlike screens.
Drone of a lustrous vailx manifesting itself
Amidst the shimmering crimson of growing colonnades;
Vibrant, luxuriant threshold burning with the sphere's dulling halation,
Solidity of its uninviting gleam absorbing the riotous tapestry
While poised motionless in the gentle patter
'neath the forest's prismatic beams.
Hovering magnificence deflecting the bright plumage flashing
As feathered tribes of plush fronds scatter in the dense verdure,
Winging towards the avalanche of blossoms
Tumbling jubilantly from the boundless azure...

Glittering spray of ferns cloaking the trill of the lush kingdom,
Rain-beads on a lizard's cryptic fabric astir on twining stems of green fire.
Tongue flicking at dragonfly tints as a snake uncoils its patterns
At the crackle of approaching footsteps in the tangled mass of deadfall.
Writhing vapors like ghosts creeping among the darkly growing treetops,
Cautious strides in the pillared labyrinth of a fear-dilated eyescape.
Heart throbbing with a sense of being watched from shades of emerald,
Stalked from the mist-enshrouded lair of a tropical specter.
Streaks of sunlight filtered through the dense canopy rent with piercing cries,
Glister of amber in the haunted wood draped with seething vines and creepers.
Jewel-feathered wings darting from limbs of moss-patinaed trunks
While passing the heady scent of blooms on sodden, rotten logs veiled in lichens.
Primitive vertigo on the shady, acidic path with giant leaves falling silently,
Skin prickling while engulfed with the humming of a hive disturbed.
Gaze electrified by the baleful glare perceived through gaps in the foliage.
A silvery-golden luster flecked with dark, mottled leafage.
Howling monkeys scrambling around the periphery of its muted grandeur
Defying perspective in the fantastic bowery of this primeval beauty.

Polished shell-beads adorning the sun-bronzed daughter
Breaking the spiders' iridescent webwork on sparkling, dripping boughs.
Eyes fastened upon the gleams distorting the feathery ferns
When petrified by the aluminous flash among the trunks,
Delicate molding of silver gliding behind the fruiting trees,
A shining apparition stirring the sickly perfume
Of variegated orchid festoonery dreamily cascading.
Fleeing into shadowy ancient aisles carpeted with velvety patches,
Sibilant whispers calling from the flickering of the verdant arboreal crowns,
Straining breath pursued by a reflected glint in the depthless ranks
With myriads of birds falling like living jewels
Upon the pungent litter when paralyzed by a lightning lash...

Exhaling forest duff burning faintly in the nostrils,
Floating with a strange immobility in the majesty of a living brilliance
Across the proud heights of rich, reddish sentinels,
Being pulled towards the gleaming carapace invading nature's dream,
With the sun's glorious irisation glancing on its metallic finish.
Penetrating the flaring colors of the forest's magical radiance,
Barbarous trunks enrobed with odorous deliriums
Of thrusting plants in a flurry of rainbow shudders.
Falling into the fluid, silvery magnificence with a thrilled dizziness,
Blurred treeshapes reflected on the hull's mercurial sheen
With patches of the tranquil sky peeking through leafy overhead screens,
Verdant fronds curtaining the terrifying complexity within.

Phenomenal green jetting into the blear of a distinct threshold,
Passing through the intolerable shining with a tingling sensation.
Retching a sickening metallic bile on a flange of latticed silver,
Now thirsting to drink the fragrant balm of the miasmic deeps
Viewed through transparent panes bordering a marvelous beveled dome
Before the steamy jungle tints vanish behind a cold, lustrous veil.
The complex pulsation of strange gemfire playing on a dirty, glistening face,
Mouth agape in the silent lucidity broken by the rattle of adorning shells.
Exploring textures with fingers that ripple the dream's luminous serenity
As the odor of fecund earth fouls the enriched glow in the corridors of eternity.
Blinking unbelieving eyes at the mystery of a rapidly dancing flame
Resolving itself into a being of cosmic artistry seated on an intricate throne,
A scintillating figure with magically swift gestures leaving a trailing radiance.
Transfixed by this mask of profound serenity caressing the heart
When jolted by flashes of the energy-specter in the penumbral tunnel
Approaching with a grotesque ballet in a forest turned vivid green by stormlight.
Infinite colors in limpid blue swimming through the brain,
An amphibious horror fabricating for itself a decorated water-matrix.

Salt-tanged lips empurpled in a shifting maze of gilded fish,
Reflective scales in an indigo abyss dreamt into perfect existence.
Flashy sheen forging in the ocean's pasture,
Jeweled, transparent wisps against the burst of anemones.
Golden minnows darting away from the shadows of menacing armadas
As eyes of vivid cobalt blue travel over the bright reef,
Frosted groves of branching coral and opaline gorgonia fans.
Macabre skeletal fingers playing shell-decorated harps
With the repetition of detail in the algal paradise unnoticed
By the Lemurian focus dazzled by clusters of varicolored enamels
While gliding through the frilled palaces of eels,
Trains of bubbles in the richly-hued gardens of tropic waters.

Rising from the enchanted depths into shoals of tinted fish,
Deafened by the thunder of crested waves in a nimbus of sunlit spray.
Thighs rippling the glittering turquoise water,
Shivering in the warmth as fiery gems cascade from full breasts.
Stainless heavens' disk of fire beaming on glaucous rollers
Tumbling upon the shore of Pan with foaming billows
As her glistening nakedness emerges from the froth of opalescence.
Lashed by pigments of royal coral and entangled with scarlet sea-ivy,
Collapsing along the tideline with the speckled clumped kelp.
Hiss of falling tide in pink earshells a-sparkle with grains of sand,
This seductive giantress benumbed by the cold pounding surf
On a powdery beach fringed with bronze-green palms.

Dripping vivid sweetness while wandering into the forest chatterings,
Gnawing treacly fruit as birds flash across cerulean patches
When startled by a figure standing among the viridescent tree-ferns.
Eyes like sapphires feasting on this beauty clothed with leafy treasures,
Ensnarled in the gaze of golden irises watching from the shadowy glade.
Whispered endearments teasing away vine-leaves from a striking physique
Before caressing her dappled bareness stretched in the emerald moss.
Blond softness beaded with miniscule jewels in the rapacious growth,
Tangles filled with dirt and twigs covering the delirium of eyelids,
Panting wildly in the green-hearted jungle, bestial grunts of exquisite agony
In the ceaseless roar of a waterfall jetting crystal in this infernal paradise.
Tongue awakening in the delicious languor of deepening hues of violet,
Ears assailed by the mewing of gulls dipping over palms of gilded fire.
Alone now on the sacred plateau overlooking an ocean of pastel foam
Charging the shore in steep billows against a fiery-fleeced horizon.
The phantom of the dreamspell having vanished at the gate of twilight,
Leaving behind a single flower to adorn the maiden's tossed hair,
Fragile white petals placed behind the ear to trap the faint moon-spears
As the spicy fragrance of sandal wafts across her stretching allure…

Coconut palms swaying against the starred infinity,
Pulse of distant drums muffled by the jungle's ceaseless symphony.
Fearful tempo calling the jewel-eyed mask of Z'Othomogo,
Doleful wailings betwixt the cadence of night's shrill chant.
Shining prick-points of spiders' eyes in spongy encrusting fungi,
Bulbed death of harlequin toads in the moon's ensilvered cone.
Ropy, orchid-draped lianas with sticky poisonous drips,
Saplings in dreaming peace haloed by pallid blooms of jasmine.
Frogs squatting in glistening pools of canopy-sifted beams,
Croaking in the prismatic slime of dark mangrove thickets,
Leaping from the brackish hues as the menacing beat quickens,
Sending leathern-winged bats into the purple evening.

Grass-girdled hips undulating to the pounding of shark-skin drums.
Lyrically moving hands veiling the faces of the dancers
Engarlanded with crimson blossoms of frangipani.
Intoxicating scents while cavorting around fluttering bonfires
With sparks like brilliant orange gems showering the palm-tiles.
Torch-swirling paroxysms in the star-arched festivities,
Devotees of the cult of the turtle-gods chanting,
Seated on greasy bamboo mats in the moth-choked blur,
Feasting on roasted black pig and branches of perfumed fruit.
Jungle's vibrant colors in their glistening black pupils
Dilated by the fire of spiced milk in muddy ritual drink.

Wizard-priest with full body tattooing draped in a feathered cloak,
Complexity of a living star-chart on a platform of vine-strangled blocks,
Seeking communion with the gods from the luminous black skies,
Raising a palm-stick scepter under the sacred alignments of space-marks
In glowing nacreous lamps as the perfumed oil of snakes scents the Mass.
Priestess without stir under a system of black mirrors,
The magician vibrating invocations while attempting to establish contact
As the dreaming mind focuses the star-king onto polished obsidian.
Fluttering swarms lit by torch-beams as the prayer-picture takes its flight,
Dream-winged from her trance-reverie aureoled with gold bristling hair.
Receiving the influx of the stellar calabash while lying on the pelts of cheetah,
Jangling with refined rapture as the compelling drums sleep.
Sorcery of tongue milking the secret eye as the generator of images twitches
With spasms of unbearable pleasure from each masterful caress,
Projecting bewitching shapes that appear in the speculum's oblique angle,
Indistinct forms confusing the reflection of her face's enchanted paint,
The eidolon gathering intensity from the glistening sweat of their effort,
Wine of lustral dewfall collected from the glands of passion.

Fantastic vividity of masks in sparkling gusts of incense,
Manifesting in the volcanic glass radiating an intense magenta iridescence.
Glittering flurries pelting the delights of flesh,
Musky bouquet of bodies curtained with rosy, nebulous drifts,
Writhing with hideous joy in the smoke of precious gums burned.
Pearl-dusted lids quivering in the fever pitch of erotic frenzy,
Moonlit seraphic eyes in the ecstasy of the serpent flame
As the reflected image arises in fumes of glowing aromatics,
Entrancing shapes of the totem pillar descending upon her ecstatic sighs,
Climaxing with ribbons of pulsating colors limning feminine curves,
Naked on variegated skins against the spangled radiance
With basaltic prisms towering against the yellow moon.

Fetishes with eyes a-twinkle in the crackling fire-bark,
Ribbons of flame on a barbaric gong sustaining the mystical revel.
Moon-silver tracery of the temple's cyclopean stonework
Shadowed by the 'spendent plumes of wings unfolding,
Blotting out the starry flickers over the billowing forest.
Disturbing harmonic of spectral bees filling the jungle's frozen tableau,
Vortex of flame-lights exposing the tiger's patterns
Patiently stalking in the sectored colors of the witch-storm.
Clarity of windless palms in the shifting light-falls,
Vegetation fanned out 'neath magnetized basalt crystals.
Sorcerer's paradisial flesh among the vailx's warped reflections,
Winging-forth to the rainbow throne on lustrous pinions.

Leaping starward in the painful brilliance of a filamentous portal,
Shedding the fleshy veil to cross an abyss of radiance.
Leaving feculent trails in galaxies receding in a blurred instant,
Paralyzed by the dread majesty enthroned within the skull's brittle envelope,
Revealing the initiating sigil graven in a royal cave of multicolored gleams,
The glyph in fields of crushed sugarcane alight with bright meteor plumes.
Resplendent canoe piloted by kings across the noble firmament,
The gateway to the reaches in an infinite expansion of pink.
Ornate locks breached with arcane caresses in the perfume of glowing coals,
Charming the pulsing blood of the decorated wand with its applied pigments.
Dark kisses awakening the sleepers from their glittering star-webs,
Shifting pageantry of the throne of ecstasy possessing the earringed one
In the aligned spectrum where gilded masks exhale the effluvia of aeons,
Attracted by the flicker of demon pearls spilled upon her sabbatic glamour,
Plunging from delicate shades of mauve with each luxurious moan.
White austerity of an angel unfurling a scroll with a foreboding aura,
Dazzling swiftness of a jeweled comet appearing in the exulted skies,
Passing with a brazen-throated trumpet's alarming blast,
Fragmenting the chilling spectacle burning in the lush undergrowth...

Woven plumes of birds shaking the dew from flowery moss,
Scattering in the dappled treetops arched with a vivid palette
As a sudden rumbling sways the translucent blue sky.
Poisoned blooms of the fire-goddess choking the giant forest
With incandescent lava flows snaking in those fabled eyes
That last glimpsed her green loveliness.
Scorched butterflies littering mosaicked courtyard plazas
With ornate pillars toppled in pools of blood.
Speckled eggs cracking in the drooping purple of sunless ferns,
Fiery trickles meandering to hiss with cascades of roaring opals
Tossing flaming pirogues laden with platinum coffins
Swallowed by the glowing magma of the prophetized
Cataclysm.

In Ancient Moonlight, the Glimmerings of Luciftia, an Atlantean Brain

'Neath a pastel-streaked sky comes the tumble of unresting surf,
Charging at the glistening shore as a faint moon slips through the dulling clouds.
Gathering sea-bleached shells am I, as the spume hisses around my ankles,
  Washing softly over the path of footprints on the tide-marked sand.
Orange-tinged foam spatters as I dash across the purple mottlings of clumped weed,
My child's fair form wet to the thighs as I slosh into the wrack-beaching swells,
Wading deeper into an ocean aflame as a melodic call in the gathering dusk I hear.
  Mingled with the crying of gulls, this trill of haunting beauty I follow
  Into over-carried spray as breakers engild the sparkling rocks,
  My answering smile tasting the wave-crests' sharp and salty sting
  'Till enveloped by billows a-glimmer with rose-tinted fire.

  From the slippery outlying rocks, I scan the horizon's afterglow,
Bewitched by the creature's song-wail, so dulcet and sweet the seraphic quaver,
  Unlike the pips and squeaks of porpoises this pleasant warble
  Drifting nearer with each breath of the rushing surf.
Filling my lungs with the pelt of spray, I dive into the moon's ensilvered flame
Flickering with sequined gleams on tidal swells flecked with breaking foam.
  Under the churning surge, I swim in turbid lunar beams,
  Hearing thrilling whispers more inside my head than with my ears,
  Impelling me to glide with arms as wings into the eerie glimmer
  Of the fucoid-robed depths reflecting the bright rising moon,
  With its glittering mass of pasturing fish dappling the sea-forest canopy.

Moving through the entangling blades, I descend upon a jumble of stones,
With fields of blooming algae sloping gently away into worlds muted and greyed.
Feeling with cold clutching hands, I move across spongy humps and bumps,
  Passing spectral faces watching from their burrows within,
Hiding from the moon's veiled glow, spilling through the hangings of weed
  Where silhouetted shapes circle, snapping at flashes of ghastly luster.
  Skimming the seabed's lurid richness, I enter a salt-encrusted labyrinth
Of monstrously-barnacled columns of stone coated with a velvety blur of mosses.
Slipping easily through this rocky chaos, I halt and hang with attentive ears
  When suddenly the water is disturbed by the skittering of bleary fish
  Agitated by the pleasing drone vibrating bones chilled to the marrow.

All at once the featureless void becomes a harlequinade of color
As there appears through the maze of rockiness a luminous corridor of sorts
Enringed with a glorious complexity of lights fluctuating with pulsations
Casting a spectrum of strange glares on the gardens of frosted coral there.
Transfixed by this hypnotic lamping, there I float, serenity enwrapt
As the sand-clouds settle to further reveal in the limpid depths
A tunnel of firmed bright water framed by an enchanting riot of ocean flora,
A tapestry of golden-brown and olivine bedizened with sponge and gorgonia,
With a rainbow of brittle stars dotting a seabed varied with patches of anemones
And pinnacles of stone festooned by sea-tangle cast adrift,
Floating aimlessly over a wilderness ablaze with encrimsoned algae.

With each flash of strange heat, my eyes could plainly see
The kaleidoscopic flurry of fish hanging motionless in a train of stilled bubbles,
Their roving shadows appearing as dark patterns fixed on the gleaming grey mud
Where statue-like, too, is the maddened scuttle of thorny sea-spiders
Stirring up plumes of living ooze from the mollusk-eaten floor;
These clouds of milky iridescence with their light-frozen swirls and twirls
Encircling a bronze whaler in whose flaring jaws its writhing prey pauses
While exuding spurts of blood in a jetting dark haze of rich emerald green,
Each drop having come curiously to a glistening stop
While raining down upon the delicacy of sea-lilies draped in sunless slime,
Every detail now startlingly clear while suspended in the spell.

Pulled slowly through the water as if drawn by some mysterious force,
I feel the sheen of the amphibious herds brushing slippery against my bare chest.
My gaze entranced on the luxuriant portal with its curving translucent walls,
Inside which appears a holy man-fish whose face is ensphered by a radiant gloriole.
Arrayed in myriad tinted reflections, I behold the majesty of its gestures,
This as the kingly-irised hues of its oddly-slanted eyes sing to me
With upsweeps in pitch like the siren's jeweled tongue I earlier heard
Beckoning me from the surging billows as a pale moon rode the twilight clouds.
Now as the ocean's variegated brilliance rushes vividly past my fluttering eyes,
I pass beyond the shell-blurred gates in whose timeless halls I glimpse
Wonders seen only in dreams behind a child's softly curtained lids.

Warmed by feelings of beatitude am I, as I peer out with half-focused eyes
At ribbons of sparkling dust among infinite nebulae billowing,
Startled now and then to see pulsating blobs flashing away like comets,
For only then do I realize this vast gulf of space lays a great many fathoms below
In a tortured landscape shrouded by phosphoric blooms of microbial floc
With brine-stained wonders cloaked with growths slithering with ophidian terrors
As nightmarish phantoms spring up out of the black oblivion,
Prowling hulks feasting on the bursts of their quarry's cryptic glory,
A garish circus of miniature dragons ablaze and a vivid carousel of sea-horses
Painting the turbulent darkness with acrobatic spirals of luminescent fire
'Till flitting noiselessly away from dim-glimmering monstrosities.

As I shrink away from the abysmal horrors seen through the clear panes,
The beasts of the deep start to fade until there's no longer a trace at all,
But now only a smoothly-polished, metallized surface where they once stirred.
Still in a daze, I turn to find myself standing in an eerily quiet place,
A scintillating white room, grotesquely sterile, with curiously-rounded halls.
Feeling dizzy by the lack of angles, I reach out to touch the pearly glistening
As I walk through this dream, confused by unimaginable things
Such as the sheen of pedestalled chairs that blend perfectly with the floor
And the smooth monotony of panels curving round the seat's contoured arms,
With the shifting mosaic of glows I bump causing colorful icons to appear
On maps of glittering infinitudes projected onto the darkening walls.

Playing with the metallic fabric of a chair grown from the floor's luster,
I turn towards an airy swish, catching a glimpse of several tall, slim forms
Approaching in a synchronized lightning-fast ballet of silver.
In the rustle of their shimmering flutter, I'm hustled down a glowing corridor
Into a smoothly-domed room whose latticed walls radiate a misty white fluorescence.
There I'm laid on a padded table that molds around me in a wondrous way,
My body soothed and tingling as I breathe the room's resplendent vapor
When, soon, I perceive in the hazy glow a masterwork of nature.
Tall and thin glides this lord of dreams with a face of calm, mysterious beauty,
The shadow of its splendor flooding me as it bends over in a ruffled collared robe,
Tranquilizing as a lullaby with movings liquid and graceful.

With the electrified poke of fingers moving rapidly over my prickling skin,
I taste in my throat a sterilized flux as it palpates various anatomical sites
'Till focusing its attention on the unmistakable flicker of fear in my eyes,
Calming me with an empathetic gaze as I stare at the disturbing artistry of the face
Moving against a clinical radiance which makes me feel dirty and ashamed.
The albinistic tones of its complexion contrasted by its bright golden-hazel eyes,
Flecked with tints infinitely more beautiful than those of mortal birth,
The deep penetrating stare of which seems to pick up my very thoughts,
For as I'm about to ask the robed figure's name in my little girl's voice,
My head fills with a musical lilt, the answer which I sought.

Unable to stop gazing into its eyes, I try to fight their glaring pull
As part of me floats above the table with the other half still locked in a mental struggle
While riveted to the glint of its pupil, a narrow slit in the iris's glistening fixity,
Dilating from a barely visible vertical crack to a widening circle of intense black,
This speckled portal I pass right through as the theater's white borders melt away.
Flexing my nostrils in the stygian dark, I still inhale the sickly-sweet fumes,
But now also dank, acrid earthen smells as two worlds become strangely intermixed
As indistinct shapes grow luminous, shadows dance on the jagged walls
In this echoing stone passage dimly-lit by a trembling reddish-orange glow
Whose source I move towards, feeling the grit of pebbles in my soles,
Pausing to pick bits of quartz from the ghostlike lavender of my feet.

Passing under rough-hewn arches, I continue through the rock-tunnel,
Straining to hear oddly-muffled spell-songs over the crackle of smoky torches
While creeping down lichened steps trickling with water echoing hollowly,
Descending into the moistness of a circular grotto lit by the twinkle of numerous candles
Set in flame-licked niches all around the dripping limestone walls
Adorned with the velvety patina of time, weaving patterns on sparkly-veined rock.
Through drifts of illuminated smoke, I discern robed and black-cowled forms
Seated reverently around a great table, their faces reflecting monastic calm
In the gleam of goblets and salvers, a vision too splendid to be entirely real,
With the assemblage oblivious to my footfalls, or to the pale apparitional face
Observing this brilliant banquet as a disembodied spectator.

In the fragrant drifts of censers turned green with ornamental auras,
I move towards the feast-table, glimpsing the bloodless pallor of dark-hooded faces
Intoning the perfumed script from the holy scrolls of kindred rebels
While seated in carved and gilded chairs cushioned with a patchwork of noble mold
In the banqueting-hall of this subterranean palace encrusted with mineral riches.
Or, perhaps, a cave-temple is this, filled with a galaxy of wax-lights
Blazing fiercely in my dazzled eyes, half-entranced by the solemnity of the Mass.
The spell broken at the concerted signal of a bell rung by a cloaked form,
Whereupon there enters the glimmering flow of a lady of startling beauty
Clad in filmy sea-green draperies trailing behind her bare sandaled feet,
A pageant unto herself with the train of lustrous silk drawn along.

With this fluttering gown clasped by brooches of nacreous shell,
She glides like a mistress of tides in whose shimmering folds the billows comb,
Her smooth curves well-defined beneath the diaphanous stuff
With braceleted arms gleaming like tarnished silver dapplings on moon-struck water,
As do the 'splendent horns rising from the band settled upon her arched brows.
But even with all her rich adornments, what most held my rapt attention
Was the austere splendor of that face peering from behind the dark gauze,
Flawless as polished alabaster, the pale skin her veil partly shrouded,
The fine lineaments a pallid mask bathed in a fountain of moonlight,
With the bronze-gold plaits framing her cheeks enhancing her petrifying charm.
This strangely-stiff profile opaquely-white in the tallows' radiance.

As she gracefully crosses over to the celebrants of the sacred feast,
Slender fingers flash begilt rings from the loose drapery of her winged-sleeves.
Yet, shaming these lovely trifles is the precious vessel held between her hands,
Its filigreed stance wrapped in tissue like a gathering of pearly cloudlets
In the midst of which it appears to float before placed on a thin slab of jacinth
On shining white linen next to the luster of the other hidden hallows
Beaming prisms in the marvelous effulgence of the service's countless tapers.
Choking on swirls of burning balsam, I watch, completely absorbed by the sight
Of this exquisite chalice of shining white bronze banded in richly-chased gold
On which flame-patterns dance, directing my gaze to the inlaid ornation
Of the starry belt of the circling zodiac crowning its glancing rim.

Leaning forward to better observe the cup's richly-wrought surface,
Piercing sapphire eyes travel over orichalcum plaques engraved with stellar monsters,
The visitations of the cloud-borne Ones insculpted in minute detail on inlaid sections
With their fireships seen descending from the lofty, starry regions.
Beneath these blazing spectacles, fabulous beasts rise from the sunless sea,
One Triton in marked relief, Lord EA., enthroned in his court of muted elegance.
Also depicted there is the account of the race of men his jewel-jetted scepter endowed,
Those molded from the clay of the earth mixed with the blood of the cosmos.
As I view this imagery of a paradisial idyll, meteors of fire fall upon the delicate tooling.
Not shooting stars of celestial refulgence, but, as I quickly come to realize,
The flying sparks of incense cast upon glowing red-hot coals,

While eternal salamanders bask in the inferno's quenchless flames,
I lift my gaze to the company of men wreathed in the thurible's azure coils.
From the shadow of their cowls, fixed, unwavering stares watch in complete silence
As this woman in her wraith-like drapery drew aside her gossamer veil
So that a rare scent wafted about her, not unlike a freshly-opened rose.
With her features now laid bare, I'm confused by a feeling of familiarity,
Like looking into a fantastic mirror is this, despite the allurement of her countenance.
And then I know I'm not merely the twig of the same tree, but, in fact, she is me,
Or, how one day I shall be when tall and superb as a mystical bride,
Full-breasted and gem-bedecked in the glorious vestments' long loose folds,
Brilliant and horned with glamour like a daughter of the night.

Inspecting the brethren's faces, I notice one of the diners abstaining,
One unlike the others stationed at the table that appears still in the bloom of youth,
The violet fire of eyes under the cowl, a sign denoting his high-birth.
Absent from the embroidery of his fine-spun napkin is the glint of eating utensils;
There's no basket of perfumed fruit or platter of peacock-rich victuals,
No goblet of aromatic foaming wine or bread kneaded from royal golden flour.
With his highly-prized gaze fixed on the priestess in her matchless sea-green gown,
She lifts an amethyst-tinted bottle of rock-crystal like those for flowerdrops
And pours into the white-bronze chalice a dark crimson fountain,
Staining the ornate cup with blood-red gold like that on her opaline nail-lacquers,
Elixir of living flesh ritually collected in the adjoining secret chamber.

As the sacrament is made ready, to the blue bewilderment of my eyes,
The saintly cauldron flashes with a blinding glare as if lit by a sunbeam
Of such penetrating brightness that it dimmed the candles' amber luminance.
Striking the jewels bordering the chalice, the feasting-hall is filled with wondrous hues,
The gems of planetary rays playing on the faces of all those witnessing the holy drama.
After the heavenly liquor is set alight, I watch an initiatory rite revealed to few
As the royal wine is ladled out into a smaller vessel with a white-silver dipper.
This drinking-cup the priestess offers to the youngest of the priestly order,
Which, when lifted, casts a jewel-radiant sigil on his robe's black draping.
After quaffing to the dregs this extract of glowing lunar essence,
Scarlet dribbles from the lips of this Prince of Darkness fed divine starfire.

With hot flares dazzling my eyes, the ceremony phases in and out
As all in the murmuring circle become still as statues in the pulsating silence.
Watching this disturbing tableau, I feel a dizzying sensation of motion,
The paralyzed pageant fading as I move through the dream's turning doors.
Looking up at the vivid golden-hazel irises directly over my face,
I blink dazedly at the glorious robed being staring down with lidless riveting eyes.
Hearing the shuffling of feet. I glimpse others in the tingling haziness,
The abstract purity of dolls in lustrous suits holding cold winking devices,
The glinting sterility of which I taste in the intense white of the Spartan theater
As a lance of diamond-light moves over flesh glazed with sparkling jelly.
Before even flinching, my fear is alleviated with a serenity rarely felt,
Calmed by the sublime texture of a hand placed over eyelids fast-shut.

While floating in the vivid luxuriance of a rippling watery matrix,
I'm suddenly thrust into the stinging brine of the ocean's delirium of colors,
Skimming a dense carpet of anemones teaming with a flitting and fluttering menagerie
Of fish poking around the voluptuous bouquets and starbursts in time-frozen flashes,
Their steel-grey undulations fixed 'till the spell is broken by a sudden rush of motion.
With platinum bubbles clouding my vision, I swim across the algae-enveloped depths,
Over sponge-encrusted rocks astir with snouts of lantern-eyed death
And puffs of gelatinous stuff rising like opal umbrellas in falls of marine snow.
In the murk of this bacterial flurry, I pass the blur of varicolored schools
'Till bobbing in the gleaming slivers above this fish-dappled world,
Watching frenzied dolphins leap against a nimbus-ringed moonset.

Salty sea-air lashes my face as I walk along the wave-licked shore,
My feet aureoled in foam as the tide falls slowly back into pale starlight.
Towards the rock-beating surf, I discern a luminous mass near the ocean's surface,
The white-crested billows trembling and roiling 'till tinged with a fantastic-colored froth.
With the waves curling over like tumbled jewels, I behold the sea-gods' titan towers
Rising from the turbulent boiling waves while ejecting a rainfall of glittering fish,
Its brilliance slowly diminishing in intensity until a beautiful perfect sphere
Tints the undersides of clouds with lights flickering dizzily around its edge.
As the oncoming tidal swells swirl around me with a greasy iridescent tracery,
I notice diffuse patches of a jellied film on the glistening tideline,
The beach strong with the resplendent stench of its awful grandeur.

As the rumbling, billowy mass ricochets with prolonged livid flashes,
Floating down from this hovering storm of unearthly hue are shining metallic strands,
Ribbons of ephemeral fluff which vanish at the touch of my numbed fingertips.
With each flaring cloud above, I've haunting flashes of the last hours
When the threatening conjunction of stars plunge Atlantis 'neath dust and wave.
As fiery grievous hail falls on vast pillared halls of polished marble and onyx,
Gilded cupolas are pelted with a shower of sand and stone,
Their palm-studded lanes turned to seas of blood afloat with purple gore.
As sun-bronzed bodies stain the turquoise water, shimmering opalescent fleets burn,
With crystal machines and flying horses entombed in a deluge of magma
And falls of ash that shroud the gloomy specter of a dull copper moon.

Startled by a shell-trumpet's blast, I awaken with my heart beating fast,
The phantasms dreamt still vivid in my mind as are the visions of ruin and death.
Turning to behold golden pinnacles against the fading celestial palette,
I knew the awful hour hadn't yet struck when the magical empire crumbled and fell.
The furious hissing of lava belched was only the swashing of pulsing tides,
The palace I beheld fathoms below, the shelter of abalone and marlin,
The columns of its elusive splendor, turrets of salt embedded with morbid shells.
Yet, seeming so real was the ensanguined talisman of the goddess enfleshed,
With its stainless recipient kings riding brazen chariots on constellations paven.
As I picture those eyes of violet fire in the watery paradise of EA,
The vision is shattered by the blare of a conch signaling the kindled dawn.

Spectrophilia

(congressus subtilis cum vas spirituale)

Multitude of angels escalloping opal eyelids
with silver-throated trumpets
banishing the hemorrhage of the ever-shifting pageantry;
dolorous phantasms of a candle's amber radiance
dancing tempestively on an iridescent thumbnail...
Unwavering.
Perfumed rose-gold flame of the luxurious night unrolling:
encharmed, prismatic flame resolving itself with autoerotic sorcery
into an alabaster countenance diademed against a tapestry of jeweled starlight.
Austere beauty, virginal purity
with the delicate lineaments ephemeral like a thurible's ghostly arabesques.
Sapphires of furtive passion gazing at he breathing the saintly fragrance,
those modest eyes kindled
while returning caresses in the glittering stellar drift.
Folds of embroidery fallen in midnight blue fretted with starry gold,
Curves of ivory rapture upon the desert's engilded sand.
Roseate breasts a-spread while kissing her honey-sweet flesh,
Fingers in coppery tangles spreading empurpled wings divine.
Amorous ecstasies on a harlequin lionskin in the impearled black,
Gemmed love-spasms 'neath the palm-jetted moonrise,
Climaxing with the Nativity of the vision's harvest,
Stainless aspiration to father the scepter of treasured hearts.

Netjeryt

Torches flaring in the dust-laden gloom
As eyes grow accustomed to the strange gleams perceived.
Engulfed in splendor undisturbed by thievish hands
In the dim flickering glow of a spacious burial chamber.
Jackal-headed deities casting shadows upon plastered walls,
Effigies of gold and black watching vigilantly from plinths.
Details of tomb murals exposed by ribbons of flame,
Red ocher profiles facing death's horizon.
Tableau of the afterlife painted from the royal palette
'Neath columns of hieroglyphics carefully executed.
Anubis weighing hearts against the feather of Maat
On the great pan-scales in the judgment hall.
Ibis-throated scribe recording the verdict
Before the deceased is led to the Osirian crook and flail.
Pillar-scepters of a purple canopy bejeweled with stars,
Cedarwood boat in the cold brilliance of perpetual lamps.
Beatified souls ferried to the distant glimmer of Orion,
Through the gates of the celestial realm of the blessed dead.
Statues of kilted mace-bearers guarding bolted doors,
Cobra frozen in gilt reflecting the trembling orange light.
Glare of a hammered gold-foil shrine with embossed designs,
Glorious winged-disk with a prismatic shimmer.
Pounding hearts wading through the clutter of regal treasures,
Heaps of dusty artifacts beaming numinous auras.
Musty pomp of sepulchral gifts in varnished coffers,
Palm fronds on tables of offerings in the palace of eternity.
Blue ice of diamonds on the pelts of leopards,
Smudges of lampblack on the pigments of alabaster.
Fruit preserved in honey in lavender-colored glass,
Bouquets of withered flowers in the house of the double.
Protective goddess with wings outstretched,
White limestone sarcophagus draped with spangled linen.
Vignettes of funeral texts on a mortuary stele
Inlaid with amulets to ward off those who plunder hearts.

Harsh grating sound as the lid is carefully pried loose,
Removed by excavators in the hushed gloom.
Inner coffin profusely decorated with vivid scenes,
Formula that enable the deceased to prevail.
Equipped spirit navigating the divisions of the nether-world,
Wadjet eyes repelling its parade of baneful specters.
Breathless anxiety as the flaking, gaudily-painted cover is lifted,
Revealing the serene, placid effigy of an ancient queen.
Head of the Pharaoh's daughter supported on an ivory pillow,
Beheld by those choking on a sickly sweet effluvia.
Unflawed calm of eyelids adorned with the glamour of malachite,
Lustrous tresses netted with turquoise beadwork.
Fillet of the royal Uraeus banding brows lavished with antimony,
Fire of the serpent's jeweled eye in the cold depths of the tomb.
Luster of royalty decked with floral garlands,
Scarlet poppies, berries and hyacinth petals.
Arms folded across her breast shaped with linen pads,
Fingers stained with henna enclasping a brittle roll of papyrus.
Swirling golden particles of suspended dust,
Rubric of the scroll crumbling at the hand's slightest touch.
Faint reflections of the queen's exquisite death-mask
In the bronze solar disk of the Mirror of Hathor.
A fine specimen of the grave furnishings to be catalogued
Among the many antiquities of the royal necropolis.
Discolored beauty of her painted features
Blurred in its patinaed surface like that of a rippled pool.
Visage of perfect serenity framed with abundant vivid black hair
From which wafts the cloying of perfumed oils.
Amber of scented breath on a face glistening with salty runnels,
Obsidian pupils dilating as the torch sputters.
Sun-lashed eyes dazzled by abrupt flashes in the polished depths,
Shifting pageantry against a blinding horizon.
Sand peopled by shadows with colors shimmering in the heat,
Babble of tongues from the ancient land of Khem...

Soughing fans of peacock hair held by bearers
With shaven scalps like polished ebony.
Pectorals of goldwork glinting against dusky flesh
Of Nubians gemmed with beads of sweat.
Leisurely enjoyment of a slender young queen
Censed by thuribles while stretched on a divan of zebra-skins.
Beguiling royal eyes painted with a kohl-stick,
Shaded by an awning of striped vermilion and gold.
Silky flowerlets on the steps of a stone landing-stage,
Quay along the green gleaming of the river Nile.
Scarlet sails a-flutter on gilded masts
Of pleasure barges with keels of rich citronwood.
Majestic swans under flame trees lining the banks,
Feathery palms reflected in the lapping water.
Queen of Khem without blemish in the fire of dripping pendants,
Carved ivory comb in her Egyptian coiffure stiff with pomade.
Filigreed diadem with asp coiling from her brilliance decked,
Azure moon in the luster of torques round her divine neck.
Wisps of transparent linen revealing pleasant curves
Of reddish-topaz with a hint of a woman's sable patch.
Scarab of agate hanging between ripe breasts
Whose nipples are tinted with carmine.
Jangle of bracelets while lifting a shining goblet,
Beer red with pomegranate juice to quench sun-parched lips.
Shrill piping of reeds by dappled musicians
In the drowsy sweetness of olivine beams.
Rigid etiquette of serving-maids girdled in saffron,
Placing before her fragrant lap a platter of burnished metal.
Delectable figs, pickled meat and green almonds,
Bunches of grapes in wicker to tantalize the nostrils.
Cool wine from earthen jars sealed with plugs of ruby-colored wax,
Clustering of flies on white cheeses of goats.
Emblems of sovereignty on a tiered scepter,
Black leopards with eyes like RA's yellow diamond.

Sacred chord sustained in lavender-blue twilight,
Silhouette of pyramids in the lingering afterglow.
Screech of desert owl beckoning from the red highway of Amenta,
Song of beetle adorned with a pale sprinkling of stars.
Whiff of lion-dung from the straw of regal stalls
Mingled with the perfumes of basalt censers.
Muddle of iridescent robes passing columns of a portico,
Roofed courts silvered in the moon that patterns tiles.
Torches flowering in the scented darkness,
Aromatic bugs swarming from a palm-leaf cornice.
Glimmer of breast-plates in a rippling lotus pool,
Manicured lawns of the temple guarded by sentinels.
Whisper of scarlet sandals behind copper-sheathed doors,
Amethyst cheeks of maid-servants with draperies a-shimmer.
Muted hues of cushions in the glow of alabaster lamps,
Sparks from incandescent coals in tarnished braziers.
Clusters of fruit on slabs of variegated marble,
Flagons of date-wine and sugared rose-petals.
Gauze-winged queen in a gown of diaphanous night-blue,
Plumed headdress with purple ostrich feathers.
Braids shiny with precious oils from terra-cotta flasks,
Gold-tipped plaits to match the splendor of lacquered nails.
Luxurious ornaments removed by personal attendants,
Bangle's delicate tracery with sapphire glint.
Undraped flesh stripped of its fire-delighted jewels,
Leaving only the gilded areola of pale brown teats.
Molding of noble face sponged of its thick cosmetic,
Stibium of eyelids staining a wiping-cloth.
Shaven body gently daubed with a towel of fine flax
Before her nakedness is covered in a tunic of unbleached linen.
Echoing footsteps in halls with painted friezes on chalk plaster,
Priest shorn of skull in a robe tied with violet cord.
Placing around her neck the charms of Isis,
An amulet of flint with magic spells to open gates.

Echo of portcullis slabs in a descending passage,
Complex labyrinths within the chamber of initiation.
Patter of falling sand as bolts are drawn back
To reveal a secret flight of rock-hewn steps.
Glitter of flooded passages in the cast of a draughty lamp,
Boat of cedarwood painted with the uninjured Eye of Horus.
Queen placed upon a lion-headed bier for the ordeal,
Prow of Anubis-head spearing the serpent of darkness.
Guiding the rudder through the sulfurous fumes,
Piercing shrieks of ghosts in the afterworld.
Misty purplish glow of a papyrus swamp,
Flame-glints on the tail of a monstrous crocodile.
Myriad phantasms gliding through the Place of Testing,
Night-feast of scorpions in spilled carnelian beads.
Lord of Duat enthroned in the cavernous depths,
Heart on pan-scales watched by the devourer of souls.
Registers of doom marked with a reed of colored earths,
Shining spirits escaping from the black throat of Ammit.
Creaking oars emerging from the terrifying gloom,
Beholder of the horizon in RA's golden opening eye.
Ram's horn trumpeted in the brilliance of descending rays,
Wake of rainbow-flecked foam behind the majestic vessel.
Colossal Sphinx encircled by a lake of chrysolite blue,
Sparkling grandeur of its mysterious profile.
Hypnotic eyes of the monolith focused on eternity,
Science of astral immortality codified in limestone bedrock.
Luminous flecks of pavilions reflected in bejeweled water,
Prismatic colossi dwarfing palm and sycamore.
Obelisked pillars of iridescent black,
Cartouche of kingship attesting to the glorious handiwork.
Stern of gilded barque anchored in a sequined harbor,
Sails embroidered with the emblems of the pyramidal lords.
Flaming wings of eagles soaring over roseate gleams,
Stench of baboons gibbering 'neath kaleidoscopic moons

Decorated ceilings of tunnels blackened by torch,
Secret journey of the initiate from the Sphinx's lower chambers.
Iron-doored portals and pitfalls of drop-stones,
Mazy passages to the hidden academy of the Followers of Horus.
Narrow shaft targeted on the sparkling gift of Sothis,
Dark cavity of the pyramid ablaze with stellar light.
Priests of the Draconian cult administering the rites of passage,
Anointing the priestess with the fat of the sacred crocodile.
Queen Sebek-nefer-Ra passing ornate pylons of green feldspar,
Blood of Isis in a brazen cup for the Feast of the Dog.
Emerging from the shadows into the emerald fire of Thoth,
Banquet of spiced white loaves with the gold powder of projection.
Rain of astral mead on a purple nemyss,
Bronze asp uncoiling into gemmed skies of Nuit.
Spangle-veiled goddess arched over harmony and proportion,
Reflective golden cap-stone against the pulse of the firmament.
Camels frightened by the demon-song of sistrum,
Living khu awakening in the chamber of the begilt jackal.
Glittering route to the cosmic address of the human double,
Iridescent elytra of beetle in the Field of Offerings.
Silver barque of fire crossing the mysterious district,
Punted in the nebulous splendor of the tresses of Nephthys.
Gates of Duat opened to the wings of the divine hawk,
Crowned falcon perched on the full majesty of the sun.
Marvels in his train seen through lenses of crystal.
Rings of jeweled dust like motes in a scepter's aigrette of rays.
Black opacity of the immortal abode of glorified spirits,
Dwelling place of the Pharaohs nourished on the Milk of Hathor.
Colors of wondrous lamps limning the roads to Khephra,
Royal dream of glistening ivory with thrones of obedient chrome.
Exquisite panels on catafalques with formula of tiny brilliants,
Mummies enswathed in dulled metallics faintly sparkling.
Complexity of masks nimbused with divine effulgence,
Preserved splendor in the ornamental jars of eternity.

Sepia moths in the oily smoke of flaming lamps,
Prismatic tools of the mortuary craft arranged on a stool.
Rigid, depilated beauty there behind reed curtains,
Canine mask of the royal embalmer aping the glorious Neters.
Cutter making a deep incision before being cursed,
Pelted with stones while fleeing into the parching heat.
Cadaverous odor as intestines are carefully preserved
With parcels of abdominal viscera flecked with blood.
Excised organs placed in jars under the protection of Horus,
Heart dripping on glazed colors while cupped in slimy hands.
Macerated grayish curds of brain scraped with an iron implement,
Extracted through the nostrils before sealed with melted beeswax.
Body cavity temporarily packed with crushed aromatic spices,
Spikenard, cassia, myrrh and cinnamon.
Removing a copper needle from a chest of crimson lacquer,
Flank sewn-up with delicate stitches of waxen thread.
Placed on a carven stone table glistening with natron,
Fluids draining as Sothis vanishes from the heavenly vault.
Pounded drugs injected to kill the larvae of beetles,
Fleshy envelope scoured with clean, pungent smells.
Leathery skin made supple with palm-wine and balsams,
Natural contours molded with linen wads dipped in scented oils.
Skull filled with medicaments injected with syringe,
Salt-encrusted tissue anointed with fragrant ointments.
Shrunken corpse besmeared with heated resinous pastes,
Black lustrous coating brushed from the steaming brazier.
Encasing the mummy in layers of gummed linen,
Geometric swathings of dyed fabrics specially woven.
Magical potency of amulets enclosed with the bandages,
Scraps of papyrus spells hidden in the breast.
Cartonnage mask to preserve the likeness of the queen,
Hues of her pristine vigor applied with the blade of a cestrum.
Hardened plaster features rouged in the House of Beauty,
Burnished replica placed over her face and shoulders.

Pale raiment of choir singing funeral dirges,
Wailing lamentations of mourners with disheveled hair.
Bright weavings of performers in ripples of heat shimmer,
Dancing fiercely to the jangle of clay tambourines.
Perfumed grease of courtiers' faces speckled with sand-flies,
Throngs reflected in the glittering facing.
Colors of the Pharaoh's bier under a star-spangled canopy,
Displayed on a sledge drawn by oxen across the dusty causeway.
Servants bearing gifts along the palm-fringed banks,
Procession of reed-floats in the Nile's burnished water.
Painted hearse in the glare of the sterile, rocky plateau
Lifted by tonsured pall-bearers in peaked kilts.
Casing of mummy raised upright in the fire-stinging sand,
Sprinkled with lustrations from an ornamental flagon.
Officiating priest in panther skins reciting glorifications,
Gazelles and antelopes hacked at the block of slaughter.
Jaws pried open with a chisel at the entrance to the tomb,
Glowing posies tossed upon the shroud by the grieving.
Friezes in the antechamber of monsters adored,
Offerings to the dead on walls painted buff like a papyrus scroll.
Scenes of the Pharaoh's entourage on the eternal journey,
Enfolded in delicate wings of Nuit's infinite richness.
Burial chamber heaped with personalia of the queen,
Cat bedecked with earrings and a falcon of polychrome.
Delights and pleasures of the ka lavishly entertained,
Ushabtiu figures of brown serpentine to perform tasks.
Ghost of heart passing papyrus-bud columns of hypostyle halls
With lamps of painted lapis in niches of gypsum.
Tempera frescoes from a slate palette's cakes of ink,
Oryxes and bubalises basking in a relief's unchanging beams.
Golden spoils of the tomb deep in shadow,
Jackal of the necropolis seal on a final coat of plaster.
Dragging a broom across the tracks of leather sandals,
Torch snuffed out while exiting the sunless passage.

Silvered Leaves of Goetic Prayers
(from the Sirian Goetia)

Enchant the blazing ruby, nimbus of thy pentacle,
Hyssop glistening face hooded in the chantry.
Seals engraved with burin in a velvet-draped temple,
Elaborate rotes within a circle scented with gilt-bronze thuribles.
Magical foci of scarlet and gold sprinkled with exorcised water,
Grimoire of black goat licked with candles' gemmed amber.
Girdle of lion's skin with eyes pale green of the Nile,
Scorpion-hilted athame tracing a star of brilliant purple fire.
Papyrus of harlequin ink from a reed of the marshy banks,
Goetic mage incanting the text by the glow of dripping virgin wax.
Sapphire lamps, oriental perfumes,
Petals of azure flowers in a gilded brazier.
A sacrifice to the angels conjured in the mirror of shades,
Spirits of the anti-spectrum embodied in the rainbow flame.
King of oils burning in chafing-dishes of silver,
Flurries of iridescence appearing in the speculum of black quartz.
Servants bound by the covenant to do the Goetic's bidding,
Directed into the Triangle of Art by the scepter of command.
Misty threats in polished stone appearing as ornate flickers,
Shod with fiery sandals from the celestial deeps.
Diademed child who teacheth with a jeweled tongue,
Pageantry of the aethyr in the black night of flame.
Violet-rayed in umbra at the pylons of Da'ath,
Crimson sun-winged angel who trumpets from opal moonfields.
Lavender desert, stellar tapestry,
Camel of the desert 'neath the aura of an ivory moon.
Reveal in the crystal scroll the treasure of the jackal,
Bread of revelation from the mill of the gleaming sepulcher.
Mummia of painted tomb whose dust prophecies,
Golden flesh of pharaoh cannibalized with the bones of twilight,
Entering the divers colors of the dragons of ecstasy.

Xibalba
(Starfire Blood-Feasts)

Aroma of chocolate, glitter of parrots,
Iguanas startled by the blare of nacreous pink conch.
Iridescent red skin sumptuously cloaked,
Mayan profile adorned with plumes of rich green quetzals.
Gleaming breastplate of turquoise mosaic,
Jeweled skull atop manikin-scepter.
Wooden trumpets leading the brilliant procession of royalty,
Parasols of bright weavings shimmering like myriad butterflies.
Copper medallions flashing among the feathers of nobility,
Flutter of sandalwood fans studded with pearls.
Colorful pageantry beneath the terraced steepness
Of a stepped pyramid-temple rising against lush emerald hills.
Richly-bedecked maiden descending the broad stairway,
Train of jade beads sparkling along the lustrous grey steps.
Bracelets glinting with the sun's prismatic flicker,
Dancing in the cerulean blue above luxuriant ceiba crowns.
Splendid headdress with an aigrette of tail-feathers,
Golden earspools shining from her reddened visage.
Approaching in all her finery from the vertiginous platform
Into the grassy plaza with gigantic stucco masks.
Drums and rattles of the gorgeous dancers massed,
Sleek black hair of choir bathed in sunlight.

Writhing bestiary, chiseled pantheon,
Profusion of macabre ornaments on the tree-stones planted.
Fantastically-carven stele casting haunting shadows
On the jungle floor trodden by obsidian sandals.
Sculptured jaguars in the sacred courtyard,
Pastel hues of temple-complexes against walls of verdure.
Monarch's radiant shield with mahogany dart-thrower,
Plumed adornment of chieftain's gem-encrusted helmet.
Priest of Kulkukan at the well of sacrificial offerings,
Beauty kneeling in clouds of perfumed resin.
Bile of maize-tamales burning in the prism of a silver heart,
Gaze transfixed at reflections in the stagnant water.
Scarlet macaws flashing in the dappled greenery,
Entwined snake of the azure moon peeking through fronded palms.
Leaves bejeweled with blossoms in delicate festoons,
Orchids and begonias incensing rain-forested bamboo.
Tall forest canopy filtering golden shafts
Glancing on effigies cast into the jade-green depths.
Maiden peering at ripples in the slimy dark cenote,
Tongue pierced with a rope of maguey-thorns.
Serene and calm face mirrored in the ominous pool,
Feeding blood to the sun at a decorated shrine.

Serene orbits in a night of milky jade,
Sapodilla-wood lintels on gleaming stucco facades.
Vermilion peristyle in faint starbeams,
Panels of the vision-serpent etched in bold relief.
Orange moonlight bathing celestial dragons on the roof-comb,
Vivid friezes with a treasure of data in intricate detail.
Jaguar-skin capes swirling in the insect ecstasy,
Drumming of turtle carapace in the terraced acropolis.
Sculptured decoration aswarm with bloodthirsty bats
Winging from the rainbow drips of ethereal magic caverns.
Masks of flayed human skin in the glow of pine torches,
Ecstatic specters in fields of pumpkins a-glitter.
Dancing in kitchen-gardens among vines of silver melons,
Venus burning bright in a diadem of floral buds.
Smoldering hearts in braziers of the feathered serpent,
Hollow gourds with fermented honey of balche.
Chanting drone in the flicker of a hidden grotto,
Mandalic quincunx oriented on the stone parquetry.
Slabs of green serpentine crusted with royal blood,
Crimson of jadeite stiletto inlaid with wizardry of stars.
Fire-macaw tufts ablaze on a ritual palm-wand,
Colorful bark-books with tables of lunar phases.
Garish altar statues in the flames of black candles,
Nodules of copal lighted from cigars wrapped in cornhusks.
Visual opulence induced by the gash of a scorpion-flint,
Scarred, variegated flesh bleeding on alabaster and onyx.
Smoking mirror wreathed with glowing gas,
Ocelot of night ripping apart jewel-feathered prize.
Hummingbird on a dais of clumps of sparkling bananas,
Painted teeth feasting by the nimbus of the moon.
Tattoos stained red from plunged stingray barbs,
Jeweled water collected in a black eagle vessel.

Black skeletons, tropical rainbows,
Aura of solar disc enthroned in clouds born of lightning.
Opalescent serpent of the ensilvered rain-musk
Awakening to the emerald heart of the world.
Dream of amethyst skull on the sacrificial altar,
Pakal falling into the maws of a florid hell.
Obsidian butterfly jetted from a kaleidoscopic garden,
Resplendent module to journey in the burgeoning earth monster.
Reclined in splendid attire among a sun-eyed apparatus,
Gemmed wristbands and ornate earflares.
Blurred paradises unfolding before the navigator's intense gaze,
Focused on eternity while at the glorious machinery of death.
Panache of Mayan royalty in cascades of star-dust,
Silken beards of corn lit by fiery green trails.
Pilotage of lustrous capsule codified in tomb vignettes,
Bright mineral paint with crocodile of the galactic zodiac.
Jeweled engine of transport swallowed by reptilian jaws,
Emitting sparkles on the flagstones of a vaulted crypt.
Lord of the jungle in a coffin painted scarlet,
Thrust into the cosmic tableau by pellets of brilliant gold.
Shroud of decayed bones sprinkled with cinnabar,
Sprouting maize in a complex bas-relief.

Gloomy forest, sunrise flickers,
Deep dense green mantle shrouded by lacy mists.
Mournful piping of wood flutes trilled by prismatic ghosts,
Fierce tropical sun sifting through the towering screens.
Exquisite bird shudders among the rain-sodden jewels,
Cacophony of indistinct multitudes scattering in treetops.
Ring of machete on a temple façade deep in shadow,
Howler monkeys in pinkish lintels hidden by rapacious ferns.
Colossal stelae engulfed by lush thrusting growth,
Chalk-white stucco portraits with grotesque heads.
Lavish monuments erected to the gods of the divine spectrum,
Mysterious figures smothered by the patter of dropping leaves.
Carven pilasters strangled by enormous roots,
Faded ebullient colors in the glistening amber of sap.
Columns of pictorial detail fallen onto the moist fecund earth,
Scarcely visible despite their lingering aura.
Panels of vivid comics veiled by traceries of moss,
Jade plaques of kings clustered with snails.
Stone of lichened staircase black with millipedes,
Rich fluorescence embalmed by jungle-covered hills.
Phantoms gliding among the rampant greenery,
Pungent fragrance of ancient pageantry.

Parsons Krater

And in the shew-stone my angel appears,
Speaks with a jeweled tongue from the depths of the sphere.
Ground the elemental with the Marrow of the Wand,
Charging the talisman for the Avatar of Babalon.

Comes a lady with flaming hair,
Sapphires those eyes of maddening glamour.
Partake the mystery with erotic alchemy,
Dreaming of a world to be.

Burn down the heavens with a treasured flame
To find paradise in the black spark divine.
Gemmed.
Apocalyptic.
Risen from antiquity with the scarlet of ravishment,
Fuel of the chalice to lift this daemonic rocket.

Call upon the aethyrs in a robe of darkness
To hide from the scorpion's gilded bliss.
Her perfumes are burnt in the moon-silver sand,
Tigress in opals of the aeon at hand.

Embrace with pleasure her defiled radiance,
Rejoice in the blood of the serpent's dance.
Partake the mystery in the opulence of silk,
Come taste the galaxies' orange-gold milk.

Quence my drouth with your navel's jeweled wine,
For there I'll find paradise in the black spark divine.
Gemmed.
Apocalyptic.
Risen from antiquity with the scarlet of ravishment,
Fuel of the chalice to lift this daemonic rocket.

Into the majestic portal of this chromatic hell
Comes a fatal indulgence to shatter the spell.
Unfolded soul's wings in a flash of crimson,
Absinthe-kissed lips 'neath the night's glittering.

Comes a lady with flaming hair,
Let your vilest ecstasy dance in sapphire.
Partake the mystery with erotic alchemy,
Envisioning the unborn One.

Burn down the heavens with a treasured flame
To find paradise in the black spark divine.
Gemmed.
Apocalyptic.
Risen from antiquity with the scarlet of ravishment,
Fuel of the chalice to lift this daemonic rocket.

Egyptian Blue Sunshine

RA,
Sail O royal barque on crimson-rayed sand
As the parched wind blows thee to Nuit's milky band.
With petrified geometry silhouetted against twilight-painted sky,
And your regal gleam entombed 'neath Sphinx's watchful eye,
Remain there hidden what thy immortal hand hath written
In tablets disturbed by hands scorpion bitten,
And torch-dripped papyrus with its magical verse
On graffitied stele and purple-shadowed obelisk,
And gilded sarcophagus graven with pharaonic curse.

O AMEN RA,
Flaxen-robed priests enter the shadow-swallowed tomb,
Pungent with the scent of sepulchral perfume,
To murmur spells from the Book of the Dead
In the lamp-flickered chamber where litanies are read.
Its cold walls ornamented with palette and reed
In jeweled scenes of the soul's passage through the sunless realms between.

Prevail! O diademed queen to whom the utterances address,
Naked on your bier with hands crossed over scarab-studded chest.
With your dark plaited hair spilled onto the limestone floor,
Let incense wing your thirsty ka out the pyramid's great door,
Through which calibrated shaft those starry beams slid,
And bathed the serene glamour of malachite-curtained lids.
With gold-flecked rays channeled to that kohled Egyptian gaze,
Appears a jackal-headed guide, the opener of the ways.
And though your royal daughter's throbbing heart is now at rest,
From the couch of death comes the faint pulse of cedar-sprinkled breath.

As a funeral drum beats to the dirge's mournful wails,
Saffron-wrapped ghosts roam Amenta to be judged on the scales.
Their weary sandals passing through the gates while in linen-shrouded sleep,
Across a river of fire are rowed by ye pilots of the celestial deep.
Triumph! O beloved, let amulet's formula protect thee from thy enemies
as revealed
in secret texts and basalt glyphs
and encoded symmetry.

O AMEN RA,

Above you unrolls the tapestry of the desert's filigreed night,
With the belt of Orion aglitter, glowing coal-like red-orange bright.
Follow in thy train, Sirius, rich with its violet flares,
In the eternal house you reach me, gliding down rose-granite stairs
'Till appearing as a 'splendent pinprick in the narrow vent,
Praise to thy fiery-darted splendor, Hathor, Sothis, Sekhmet.

Queen, your body washed in the milky-green water of the Nile,
Shaved and sable-brushed are your amber-dabbed wiles.
Coolly fragrant flesh starts to quiver as an asp uncoils and slithers
From curved hips to lips as lashes twitch with a grey-irised sliver.
Bangles, bracelets and headdress jingling with each begemmed spasm
As the serpent who danceth in blood, flameth in thy delicate pink chasm.
Your feline beauty now bedewed with the silver wine of the moon,
From head to dusty toes, a cocoon spun 'neath Nuit's sparkling loom,
With the bouquet sipped, though sweet, still leaves my drouth unquenched,
Goddess of golden-white star-rain, pour forth the beer of everlastingness.

Lift your head from glazed pillow, and with wings of glory outspread,
Take flight in the vaulted passages, lamp-smoked walls tinged dusky red.
Gauze and swathings of the pupal case are left near the varnished funeral chest
As is the mother-of-emerald amulet that flashed between thy uncovered breasts.
Raise thyself from the throne of the soul, shine forth in the kindled sky.
go quickly
from the reach of thievish hands,
chrysalis to butterfly.

RA,

On the sandy wastes shed thy bitter rays
In the gloom of despoiled tombs where obsidian eyes gaze.
She preserved in mummy-cloth and honey hath felt my burning breath,
Fluid-stained rags of canopic jars strewn with the potsherds left.
Tissue rubbed in bewitched oil hath crumbled like a brittle scroll,
Heart jelled black from embalmer's syringe as is her bitumen-steeped soul.
Yet, do not dampen those yellowed windings with tears of sorrow,
But with sobs of joy, for I have lifted the veil of Isis,
To me belongs Yesterday, I, Osiris, know Tomorrow.

The Jewel of Divine Anthropophagy

I wander in black perfumes among the ungolden lamps of Abydos
As winks the specter's head o'er Umm el Ka'ab.
I trod the purplish serpent's hiss in a cenotaph of star-arched Abjdu,
Breathing the pallid luster that shrouds those reposed in painted tombs,
Immortal souls projected into the night whose glittering infinity blooms.

With winged-sandals and leathern kibisis, I seize the trophy of gleaming Qa'a,
Hetepsekhemwy seated in the orange-gold Triangulum
(Aegyptus, Nilus, Nili Domum).
Yea! The solar barque of the Osireion, green whispers of royal Pharaohs,
Joining the eaters of the Opal of Zra'd as the terrifying demon blinks,
And riseth with glory inherited from the bread of the mastabas.

I wander amid faded vignettes into fields of cold spangled brilliance,
Shedding bandages of fine linen and gold cartonnage mask.
I pass alabaster jar-seals in shadowy torch, papyrus-rolls of the jeweled dead,
Gilding my scarab amulet with the light of the kings of Sakkara,
Death's treasure-rain in dusty turquoise pots from the variegated crypts of el-Amra.

With kyphi and myrrh for the double, I perceive its scenes with ribbons of flame,
Strong of tongue from text and formulae as worms feast on the rubric.
Hail! The iridescent gluttony of carrion-hawk & prismatic emerald beetle rolling dung,
Incorruptible the germ of the deceased, mummified in the parching heat,
Joining the lords of sparkling eternity in the horizon of Khepera.

Commentary

In the mid 1990s, a series of magical operations, ceremonial in construction, were performed by a Lodge with the goal being to trick, if you Will, the brain into releasing certain endogenous tryptamines. Using sonic and visualization techniques accompanied by 'theatricals', the mechanics of the ritual were specifically timed to coincide with the plummeting brightness of the famous eclipsing binary star ALGOL (Beta Persei). Although the blinking star is 93 light years from the earth, it was not chosen as the focus of the Working because of some shadowy connection with the Thelemic 93 Current*, nor because the variation occurs every 2.876 days (=23), but because Algol was known in ancient star lore as the Arabic *Ra 's al Ghul* (The Demon's Head), and was considered to be "the most evil, violent and dangerous star in the heavens." As "the Demon's Head", it was associated with the serpent-headed Medusa being decapitated by Perseus, from which springs the winged horse Pegasis. By using one's visualization abilities while the brightness of the variable star is dimmed (symbolically killed) during the eclipse, the hope was for the pineal to facilitate, not just trace amounts of the endogenous tryptamines, but to deliver the 'mother-lode' burst that some speculate is discharged at the moment of physical death. Another unique feature of the ritual involved projecting one's self into the astronomical constellation "Triangulum," thus allowing the 'spirit' of Algol to manifest within the experimenter (similar to the investigation of the 10th Aethyr at Bou-Saada when Crowley placed himself inside the Triangle of the Art while invoking Choronzon). Needless to say (one hopes!), tampering with neural circuitry can be a risky business (particularly when it comes to the autonomic nervous system), and the greatest precautions should be taken. With this in mind, the "Algol Rituals" were performed despite Crowley's 'warning' in Atlantis that "if you pay sufficient attention to your heart, you will make it palpitate."

* There is, however, a piece of 'fiction' by Aleister Crowley entitled "The Stratagem" which is considered to be one of the author's most accessible works, in part because the prose is not nearly as abstruse as his more esoteric treatises on the magical arts. For this reason, it is even found in school libraries. But, as with most of Crowley's writings, "nothing is as it seems." This is especially true when it comes to the ALleGOricaL Stratagem. In the story, which concerns a daring escape during an eclipse from (ostensibly) Devil's Island, Crowley mentions something called "Dodium" which he says is the rarest of known elements in the universe, and which exists only in the star γ Pegasi. Writing of this "subtle exposure of English stupidity" in his Confessions autobiography, Crowley mentions a curious incident that occurred during a Magical Operation known as "The Paris Working." Later that night he dreamt about a story "that was set in a frame of the craziest and most fantastically gorgeous workmanship." Upon awakening from these rare glimpses of Zothyrian vistas, he wrote the story down, thereafter considering "The Stratagem" to be part of the magical outcome of a ritual which involved exploring "Jupiterian phenomena" (meaning that it was designed for the acquisition of wealth). With its references to Freemasonry, decapitation, and even cannibalism, here then is a valuable clue as to the identity of true strata-gem that was 'mined' by the ancient Atlanteans (or civilization X if you'd prefer).

A Cornucopiae Between Compasses

Geometrician-builder arched o'er ensilvered pyramids,
Knotted green rope encircling jeweled chalk on apprentices' rolled tracing board.
Tapestry of All-Seeing Eye in lone glimmer, starry vault reflected in mosaic pavement,
Harlequin of Aegyptian blood climbing a winding staircase to the hidden lemniscate,
Brass tripods' violet flame saluting the Lion of Tomorrow.

Gavel and chisel impose the worker's Will on unhewn stone,
Jackals on golden pedestals; rough ashlar of catacombs
(Bringing forth the sublime horizon).
Irised grey visage cooling in a sarcophagus 'neath the royal art of measuring,
Mummy-rags saturated in honey, unbeating heart of almsbox,
Brazen pillars of unfinished Temple, chapiters of pomegranates and lilies.

Emblematic lights painted by Memphite of the Rite of the Sacred Tetractys,
Celestial reed-floats in murals o'er a frieze of black and white.
Hoodwinked at the great banquet, HE with an embroidered lambskin apron,
Consuming the mumia of enlightenment from a treasure uncoffined,
Sprig of acacia uprooted at the shadowy catafalque of this Osiris.

Scythe of infinity harvesting from a skeleton once cable-towed,
Grisly ornaments in tenebrous shades as observed from behind a papyrus column.
Veils and sulphur, ivory key, trowel and scepter,
Ruby cockerel of Re/Ptar disturbing scorpion on checkered floor,
With skull & crossbones at adjournment in the extinguished flames of azure.

Commentary

In certain temples of Ancient Free and Accepted Masons, prior to admission into the Mysteries, a prospective initiate is led into the Chamber of Reflection. Depending on the particular temple of the various Masonic federations, this might be a small room adjoining the Lodge, an imitation sepulcher of Egyptian likeness, or even an artificial grotto. Whatever the case, with its dimly lit walls painted in dark shades, adding to the sombrous quality of its gloomy furnishings, the chamber is designed to produce an atmosphere that is both conducive to serious meditation and to the conception of a transition of sorts that awaits the profane it encloses. This latter notion, that of the refinement of the individual is hopefully suggested by the assortment of curious ornaments placed there. Traditionally these are a human skull & crossbones, a chunk of bread and flask of water, saucers of salt and sulphur, a solitary lighted candle, a scythe (or depiction of the "Grim Reaper"), a hourglass, the image of a cockerel, and a sign on which is written the alchemical maxim V. I. T. R. I. O. L. U. M. (an acronym for the Latin phrase *"Visita interiora terrae, rectificando invenies occultum lapidem, veram medicinam,"* which translates into English as "Visit the interior of the earth, and by rectifying you shall find the hidden stone, the true medicine"). Seated at a table for this initial part of the first ritual, surrounded by the *memento mori* and esoteric symbolism just mentioned, the newcomer is provided with pen and paper and instructed to write his Moral and Philosophical Testament.

Before the candidate is allowed to proceed with the first stages of initiation, the Philosophical Will, with its expression of one's heart's desire, is read and analyzed in order to judge the character of the individual who seeks illumination by exploration of the Paths of the Mysteries (i.e. the key rituals of modern freemasonry). However, with regards to this starting point – a modern convention of the cave of initiation, thus reminding the aspirant of the connection between life and death…the womb and tomb, keeping in mind that the true secrets of the Order in question are admitted to have been lost, with substituted ones ("veiled in allegory and illustrated with symbols") being taught to the Brethren until such a time when the genuine secrets are rediscovered, dare we consider such a custom – this initial "trial and proof of earth" to be a corruption or dim reflection of the rites of an ancient priesthood whose members were initiated into profound realities (things not divulged by the mystai so readily as with today's worthy brothers)? Was, then, this original Will and Testament that was signed in a chamber, properly tyled or otherwise, not solely of a philosophical and moral nature, but more akin to the modern document, namely "a written instrument legally executed by which a person makes disposition of his/her estate to take effect after his/her death?"

Enhaloing the Lamanaut

Shrill whistlings of the majestic solitudes,
Titanic rocks in lavender drifts.
Snow leopard of a pale green moon enhaloing opulent kingdoms
Of steep rocky outcrops 'neath glittering white summits.
Eyes of prismatic amber watching the silver-winged dragon
Coiling and curveting against mountain walls glistening.
Deafening crash of thunder shaking alpine forests,
With sparkling avalanches rumbling throughout the range.
Ibex and blue sheep vivified on a frozen canvas
In a blinding flash of lightning from the pastels of monsoon clouds.
Pines and rhododendron lit up with a brilliant clearness,
Breathtaking grandeur of gorges and precipices intensified.
Labyrinth of boulder-strewn canyons in the mysterious depths,
Jeweled lakes of blue intense as sapphires.
Opals of brown horses alarmed in patches of green,
Neighing in dappled meadows along the high plateau.
Petrified attention of kyang in dew-gemmed grasslands,
Thunder of herds galloping under violet mountains.

Birds entranced by the aura of silver majesty
Hanging stationary in a grove of mighty conifers.
Gleaming metallic egg pulsating with a multiplicity of colors,
Humming like swarms of maddened bees in the forest primeval.
Fluidity of its radiant splendor absorbing the exotic verdure,
Coppery trunks robed with velvety lichen.
Drone of hexagonal veiling spewing cascades of molten gold
From the dulling rainbow-halo enveloping its peculiar sheen.
Mossy carpet of the wood aglow with beams of variegated fire
Flickering like bolts of kaleidoscopic lightning in the clearing.
Silvery-blue flame becoming a frail, uniformed entity,
Bodily luster of a complex doll dwarfed against the aboreal curtain.
Wandering from the sphere's mercurial surface
Reflecting in its painful harmony the mist of iridescent puddles.
Blossoming orchids and ferns in eyes of black holiness,
Rich tableau of flowers thirsting for ghostly rays of cerulean.
Entering a brilliant tunnel amid tapestries of dusky emeralds,
Vanishing from the fragile pageantry of indigo butterflies.

Muted golden images wreathed in coils of patchouli,
Lacquered tea-tables with gilt-copper censors.
Ornate lantern's glow casting shadows on the wall hangings,
Silken thankas with a pantheon of tutelaries enhaloed in flames.
Shaven austerity of an occultist in a brocaded oriental robe,
Deeply absorbed behind a lattice screen of richly-carved teakwood.
Kneeling at a magical altar redolent with temple-incense,
Spectrum of flaming oil in bowls of chased silver.
Lodge-room furnished with bookcases containing rare volumes,
Dusty wisdom of pages bound in gilded leather.
Explorers seeking the Hidden Masters of Tibet and Mongolia,
Keepers of a treasure fallen from the starry infinity.
Whispers of caravan drivers heard over patinaed camel-bells
Of a blooming oasis hidden by the desert's crimson veils.
Shifting sands revealing the golden caves of Agarthi,
Leaves of purple-inked Senzar in libraries of ancient scrolls.
Gazing at a framed portrait of a mysterious being,
Praeter-human intelligence with a bald, bulbous cranium.
Narrow slits of eyes widening in a face of leaded grey,
Almond-shaped bulbs of glistening black unblinking with a hypnotic fixity.
Ringing silence while focused on the sketch of a magical séance,
Mantra disappearing into flames of perfect darkness,
Lamanaut draped in vermilion falling into an abysmal void,
Embroidered dragons in bluish streams entwining iron scrollwork.
Visualizing the painted sigil at the gateway to initiation,
Sensation of vertigo in a corridor of many brilliants.
Stepping beyond an ornamental pylon into the perfumed azure,
Shielded from intense sun-showers by a decorated parasol.
Mind transported to a heavenly dimension of existence,
Lush paradise unfurling like a vast landscape scroll.
Poppied rainbow valley 'neath fantasies of snows,
Kingdom of Shambhala a-shimmer with dreamlike opalescent light.
Rider of a jeweled horse upon the pulse of unearthly green,
Fragrant sandalwood censing the peacock throne of enlightened kings,
Shining devas appearing in the nimbus of a resplendent egg,
Guides of the living mandala in polished golden cars.

Intoxicating gardens of blossoming flowers,
Clarity of wondrous hues in a variety of focuses.
Scent of jasmine 'neath garlands of hanging moss,
Waterfowl flapping wings, dripping gems from bluish-copper streams.
Pavilions encrusted in coral shaded by luxurious foliage,
Swans on lakes of blue silk under canopies of chiming jade.
Gilded pagodas reached by a flight of roofed stairs,
Melodious bamboo flute trilling from moonlit verandahs.
Voyager carried aloft in a globule of radiant amber
Over Himalayan pines to the abode of the holy immortals.
Stupas of turquoise against night's dazzling glimmer,
Commanding edifice of a lamasery perched on a formidable ledge.
Pungent labyrinth of halls lit with butterlamps a-twinkle,
Sickly odor mingled with resinous incense of deodar.
Monks in lustrous orange silk gliding down crumbling steps,
Leading the aspirant into an undiscovered crypt.
Effigies softly radiating in the aureole of eastern candles,
Protectors of the treasure embalmed with cinnabar.

Lamaic scepter adorned with black serpents,
Staff bedecked with the scintillant fragment of the Dropas.
Iridescence of the star-stone, Ixaxaar, held in fingers of yellow mist,
Congealed kala with sigils of the Nagas in an oily, garish vortex.
Gusts of mauve pelting the aura of the traveler
Protected by the spectral mask of LAM and a sword of mulberry.
Floating in tranquility against the spangled radiance,
Etherealized shells preserved by the elixir of deathlessness.
Astral palace in rippling sand like luminous topaz,
Charming gardens enameled with flowers yielding luscious fruit.
Regal grace of a tigress silhouetted by a moon glittering red,
Jeweled azure face of a voluptuous, heavenly nymph.
Slender-waisted maiden with firm round breasts,
Clothed in wisps of gauze like blissful violet clouds.
Hands of the apsara offering a skull-cup of celestial wine,
Silver nectar poured from the spectrum of chakras.
Drunk on the beauty of eyes the color of an unfaded lotus,
Lying supine in the glamour of a magical pencil.

Of the Unearthing of the Stolen Brilliance of Zu

Earth-splitting sun gleaming on the clinking of pickaxes,
Burnoosed Arabs like wraiths in the platinum-rayed glare.
Noisy progress as layers of time are unearthed
Under the watchful eye of a vulture circling the trenches.
Tables of potsherds, chaff and bones speckled with flies,
Remains of glazed colors in the lingering dust.
Painted bricks strewn about the mysterious flat mounds
Of once mighty terraced-towers that reached the sapphire heavens,
Now blanched with age in the scorched vastness.

Dusty precincts girdled by fences of bleached camel-thorn,
An archaeologist in his tent, wreathed in bluish pipe smoke.
Perspiring in Khaki and drab, dipping into tins of delicacies
Washed down with the velvet sting of cognac
While cataloging sun-baked shards
Of a puzzling wedge-shaped script,
Clay fragments which bring to light the cradle of civilization,
Lost cities beneath drifts of sparkling sand.
Working feverishly to meet the rush for antiquities by foreign museums
Under the suspicious eye of swarthy, turbaned officials,
Dealers in the flourishing black market trade,
Curios sold in tortuously-twisted alleys
Of lantern-lit Baghdad bazaars,
A cacophony of voices and the tuneless piping of reeds
As flame-patterns dance on carpets of glittering fantasy.

Vivid languor rent by the commotion of diggers,
Amulets of quartz flashing in the sun's blinding streaks.
Parched throats muttering protective incantations against the ill-omen
From brittle, tattered leaves of sheepskin scrawled with myrrh-ink.
Artifact disinterred from a pit where it slumbered for millennia,
Grim aura dusted with a sable brush
Revealing a canine face with gaping mouth.
Figurine of a bird-taloned monster with corroded wings outspread,
King of evil spirits of the air, Pazuzu, Lord of the wind demons.

Warding off evil with their variegated stones secreted in clothes,
Bulging obsidian eyes casting a deathly glance.
Peasants fleeing from the ancient relic
With its curse graven in a dead tongue:
For all those who crawl like beetles amongst the potter's clay
And soiled sackcloth, feeding on the dust of this gloom-wrapped nether.
Sky growing dark over the desolate plain,
Crimson sea of sand rising on the horizon
Like a distant swarm of locusts.
Spreading rapidly over the pitiless wastes 'till the flaming sun is vanished,
Clouds of demons moving with the rustling of great wings.
Muffled shouts obscured by the opaque curtain,
Reed huts and scaffolds tossed in the shrill flurries
Wreaking havoc on the encampment pelted by swirls of debris
As husks of dragonflies rain down upon the ripples of red eternity...

Dusky yellow moon bathing the ruins of the ziggurat mounds
With nomads' campfires a-twinkle in the desert twilight.
Indistinct shapes wheeling above the faintly-shadowed brickwork,
Alighting upon the doleful shades of the season's diggings.
Birds scurrying across the stratum littered with dust-laden secrets,
Exquisitely-painted jars and earthenware with carbonized smudges
Entombed by the beast of wind-borne sand.
Stifling breeze blowing the horrid perfume of carrion,
Glimmer of excavated statuary in crepuscular beams.

Magus with granite-hard features and a shaven, domed pate
Seated in a pentangled magic circle drawn on the scorpion-infested ground.
Athame in its gilded sheath reflecting the quivering candles,
Licking tongues of flame catching his robe's ample black draping:
The occultist in full ceremonial regalia gazing deeply into a Babylonian gem,
Building up visions in the depths of the shew-stone.
Ears ringing with cicadas and the camels' symphony of old brass bells,
Seer intoning the formula which opens the gates of the abyss,
Mauve shades haunted by screech-owl and jackal,
Baleful hunters of the night
Banished by the purity of he of the Middle Pillar.
Washed in moonlight, shadows flitting about the forgotten splendor,
Ghostly shapes summoned from their coldly-splendid palaces beneath.

Shifts of color acquiring definition in the heart of the sphere,
Vividly bright constructions of the magician focusing his concentration,
Steadying a lintel's reliefs as a reference point in the eternal spectrum
'Till standing before a richly ornamented portal guarded by huge winged-lions,
Lamp-flames ablaze in their faceted eyes
As the ring-bolts are unlocked.
Parquetry of floor and marvelous decorated walls,
Gilded cedarwood bordering double-doors of hammered metal
Opened on mysterious, opulent vistas veiled in sun-glare.

Shimmering, haughty palaces with turrets against the unclouded azure,
Paradises of tiger and ringdove shaded by softly swaying palms.
Luxurious hanging gardens reflected in water struck by the sparkling sun,
Umbrage of pavilions ornamented with trellising of gold.
Mosaics in waves of heat-haze passed by camel and brightly-dyed throngs
On dust-choked metropolitan streets.
Litters passing under tall bronze portals,
Sirrush-dragons on obelisks gazing down upon the wanton luxury.
Fanciful zigzags and astragal
Sheathing the walls of a luscious harem.
Sultan reclined on damask, surrounded by idolatrous splendor,
Glutted on the richness of figs and honey
Fed to his majesty by bejeweled olive fingers.
Temple courtesans in flowing, diaphanous veils,
Dancing with perfumed scarving to the rattle of timbrel.

Night's purple cloak as the citadel of Babylon blazes in splendor,
Thumping of drums shaking the glittering vault of the sky.
Snorts of a great bull sprinkled with glazed bowls of lustral water
Followed by the knife-thrusts of a stargazer,
("Bull, the guilty Zu are you.")
Blood sacrifice to atone for evil plottings in the distant past,
Ritually slaughtered animal staining the temple-courtyard's bricks.
Spilled entrails fuming in a widening puddle under the silvery moon
Like the mask of Huwawa, son of Pazuzu, whose breath is death.

Specks of the arterial spray obscuring the skryer's stone,
Gut-pile torched in a purification by burning
As the seer clears the blood-stained crystal,
Once again plumbing its vast depths with a steady gaze.
Shrouded figure in the crowd signaling with a cryptic gesture,
Leading the magician from the ornate friezes of the temple-complex;
Proxies of polished diorite gazing at the brilliant skies.
Moving through the avenue's throngs
As passersby avoid dangerous glances.
Magic charms scattered on rugs in the marketplace
Where brightly-mottled snakes dance to wooden flutes
In the pallid lamplight;
Storytellers enthralling audiences over the jangle of horses' bridles.
Moving from the street marvels, eyes travel down a back alley
When an Arab steps from the shadows, flashing a daggered smile.

Piquant fumes of hashish and prisms of cut-glass bottles,
Arabesques of the wall decoration
In the flickering of tarnished brass lamps.
Wan faces sucking ivory-tipped hoses entwining hookahs.
Seated on cushions around trestled-tables in spirals of intoxicating smoke.
Glint of scimitar hanging from obscurely menacing figures
Exchanging furtive glances in the half-light of the den's soporific façade.
Password given to a figure who answers with a counter-signal,
Lifting a sequined tapestry that conceals a secret passage.

Recognition signals shown while moving through a dark passageway,
Vapors of narcotic resin mingling with drifts of bespiced braziers.
Ushered into the resplendent hall of a magnificent inner temple,
Brazen tripods of burning aromatics on matting and sheepskin rugs.
Walls bedizened with diapered hangings and talismans
Engraved upon the seals.
Emblems of the mystical fraternity with their majestic beards of indigo,
Magi in long pleated robes
Of vivid embroidery and turquoise miters,
Offering hospitality for he who seeks admission to their path,
Sashed purple-edged royal magicians' gowns appearing in the sphere,
Itself the jewel once set in a phantom-caliph's fallen crown,
Formed of solidified secretions
Of the silver fire of a thousand Arabian moons,
Precious stone of his majesty of the Order of the Black Peacock.

Peeking through the glister of beads into the inner sanctum,
Sweet arpeggios of harp strummed from behind filigreed screens.
A woman of remarkable beauty in the diffused amber light
Rising from the luxurious comfort of silken cushions.
Sultry night pearling flesh girdled with a pubic ornament,
Sprinkling her nakedness from a gilded basin of rosewater.
Torques gleaming with gold-fire as are her bracelets' prismatic beams
While painting lids with kohl to enhance the glamour of almond-shaped eyes,
Irises of fading violet-blue that once cast the spell of Eridu.

Bearded Magi-Kings in the glow of blazing olive-oil lamps,
Voices of the wise-men conceding the deficiency of the jeweled strain,
With the poverty of royal blood swallowed into the ground,
The purer lunar essence once transmitted by a dynasty of priestesses
Having weakened over generations of kingly succession.
Now shown a powdery substance of shining metal
Held in the purple gloves of a priestly figure
Appareled in a robe of harlequin.
An ingestible substitute for the richer prize of ancient custom
When those bred for kingship
Were fed from a chalice of menstrual nectar,
Nourished with blood-red gold
Collected from the Temple of the Mother,
The potent elixir to be replaced by this iridized white powder
Baked into the bread of paradise with the ruling of mystic fire.

Secret of the divine process now in the reach of mortal men,
Attainable, the crown of perfection opposed by the watchers of the throne,
The sustenance of the kingly-line bred in the House of Shim-ti
Whose ladder of stone that reached to the heavens they frustrated,
Causing a great confusion of tongues as people were scattered abroad
After the grand assembly of gods abandoned Sumer
Like flocks of migrating birds.
His majesty's precious stuffs ablaze under walls of collapsing mortar,
Sending great clouds of dust where the mighty tower of Babel has fallen.

Fighting drowsiness as the shew-stone fills with a misty indistinctness,
Eyelids heavy from draughts of sweet wine laced with sleeping drugs.
Seeker of illumination wandering amid the fetor of dirt and bitumen,
Through a labyrinth of sepulchral urns in the darkness of a vaulted chamber.
Eyes adjusting to the glittering plunder against the limestone walls
While wading amongst the morbid gleam of the death-pit treasure,
Parasol of dingy ostrich plumage and a begilt spindle inlaid with lapis.
Haunted by a face's ghastly beauty,
Violet eyes of mussel shell gnawed by worms,
Her gold-decked torso on its funeral bier,
Swagged with a cloak of tar and pitch.
Fragility of queening tresses adorned with a tinseled headdress,
Jewel-dripping corpse laden with glamour.
Her maid-servants' skeletal remains littering the royal grave
As do the bones of silver-collared oxen pulling carts of rotting green…

Exiting the grave-shaft to a dirge of choir and muffled drum,
Passing the jingling of gaily-caparisoned horses
Pulling sledge-chariots with tassels and streamers.
Drivers leading the ghostly procession down the sloping ramp
With attendants bearing the wardrobe chests of their royal master.
Singing courtiers clothed in linen carrying bronze drinking-cups
Taking their places on woven mats at the bottom of the tomb-chamber,
Ladling poison from a metal cauldron as fingers pluck a lute
'Till silenced by layers of earth, the floor of their funeral feast.

Glaring stretches dimmed with a pulsating insect shrill,
Skryer's stone enhaloed with the dull iridescence of a brackish marsh.
Wild cattle lowing in moonlight reflected on the flood meadow,
Nakedness of brutes squinting at distant parapets.
Baggage-trains in the festal glow enveloping a galaxy of tents,
Camels grunting in the delirious festival
As decorated gates are shattered,
Revealing palaces with ivory-gilt domes flickering like mirages.
Ornamental pavement with stalls lamping on bedizened awnings,
Reek of leeks and onions on coals of braziers.
Aromatic puffs of censers on poles moving through the mephitic crush,
Dwarfed by the colossality of the ziggurat
While mounting its great staircase,
Carrying offerings to the platform temple under the heavenly vault.

Stepped temple tower reaching to night's gorgeous arch,
Viewed by fish-garbed priests through polished crystal disks.
Milky nebulosity disrupted by a fantastic spreading void,
Winged-gate of the starry abyss opening with a twisting, shifting vortex.
Highway of an astral kingdom stretching across the dark unknown,
Hurling dislodged stars with grand showers
Like mighty firebrands thrown.
Brilliant sparkling trains gloriously ablaze with dusky greenish trails
Stupefying those watching the spectacle from the terraces of temples.

Clouds flashing with lightstorms massing into a floating construct,
Silent immensity passing across the moon's borrowed clarity,
Darkening the gilding of temple-roofs
And the golden cupolas of palaces.
Phantom mass approaching, casting further ominous shadows
Upon the luster of chariots drawn by braying asses
In the crowded alleys of the city-quarter
Copper-helmeted soldiers pressed against the rampart's painted panels,
Drifting with the crowds in the tumult watched by giant basalt lions.
Hulking mysterious ship anchored above the terraced mass
Like a vast blackened bird
Dimly-gigantic against the twinkling stretch,
Blotting out the firmament of stars
Whose bright sprinkling define its borders.
Raptured expressions in the stationary glory of the handiwork of Anu.

Towering gateway ablaze with fiery beacons of the reception party,
Ritually visited by the Anunnaki from across the resplendent ocean.
Visits heralded by the celestial hysteria observed in the magic glass.
Wielder of a lion-headed scepter presiding from his sapphire throne,
Flanked by priests dressed in long pleated robes
With dorsal fins like the apkallu from the City of Fish.
Diviners studying entrails arranged on gem-encrusted platters,
Docility of leopards crouched at the sandaled feet of the Sumerian queen
Amused by the variegated faces of a troupe of dwarf-clowns.

Offering tables of a great banquet in wafts of purifying tamarisk,
Roasted meat on brass and lapis lazuli bowls of cream.
Jet eyes of a slaughtered menagerie
Sprawled on blood-moistened sawdust;
Wine of sweet dates in glazed ewers adorned with gilded straws.
Mitered priests bowed in adoration while receiving command-visions,
Star-arched portal of the gods mysteriously opening with a lurid glare.
Slaves of the priest-king bearing gifts of bdellium and onyx,
Pudgy blue face of his majesty with the sign of the stars in his flesh,
Ushered before the throne-base of Ninurta with its lifting radiance.
Scribe with reed-stylus recording the scene in spellbound silence
As those chosen for the divine encounter
Vanish from the lofty platform in a rush of brilliance.

Royal delegation transported in beams of iridescent ecstasy,
Crossing into a wondrous dream-matrix unfolding with a paralyzing tingle.
Kneeling envoy making grand gestures from the hall's luminous floor
In a sanctuary of futuristic chalk-white
With a fantastic maze of effulgent corridors.
Vague silhouettes undulating against the contour of the scintillant walls,
Gleaming being-forms eclipsing the nobility of Ur with such terrifying beauty
That the secret of Zu's true ancestry is obscured by masks of pity
Before the splendid mirror is veiled by the clouded eyes of the gazer...

Pastel shades of the Euphrates without reed-huts along its banks,
Bleak lavender dunes passed over by the winging of falcon and sparrow.
Sheep grazing in purple shadows
Without the regal dogs of shepherds
As stout, shaggy-haired figures drink with gazelle from sunset-tinged puddles.
Marshy plains at twilight devoid of painted barges punted in the gloom,
Strange brilliants in parallel strips
Dotting the fertile crescent's expanse
Seen through scattering orange-tinged clouds
Reflecting a mirage's overpowering glare.
Imposing complex of domed foliage like that of an enclosed garden,
Flourishing oasis of acacia and date-palm bearing fruit within.
Moon-dappled orchards gemmed with apples plucked by a reaching hand,
The flushed bareness of a man watched from the boxthorn and bramble
By the omniscient, inscrutable majesty of cherubim's topaz eyes.

Figure of mysterious design strolling amid densely growing willows,
Watching the nocturnal ballet of celestial steeds.
Yelps of lions growing more distinct
Outside the gates of paradise.
Distended abdomen of silver carrying within it the germ of humankind,
Man-flesh wrapped in the protective aura of the birth-goddess,
Fashioned embryo implanted in the garden of the celestial womb,
Creature of earthdust to be elevated with royal obligations
With the cutting of the umbilical cord at the moment of being brought forth.

Gold aureoled with jewelwork, a prized sapphire fallen to dirt,
The exalted tiara of Enlil usurped with a sword of brilliant crystal.
His throne smote with missiles
Proudly hurled by the rebel Zu,
Crowning himself with princely status while girt with dreaded brilliance.
"He who knows" leading the mutineers with their fear-inspiring splendor,
Having stolen the tables of scientific law from a copper tablet-box.
Dialing in a sunburst of horror
Whose direful thunder shakes the steppes,
Raining feathers of birds on blackened pebbles of the scorched plain
As niveous lambs bleat in anguish, their mouths foaming with blood.
Divine black bird piloted by the adversary god, Ninurta,
Mobilizing angels with flaming stones
To crush the diademed skull of Zu
And return the Tablets of Destiny from his cedar-perfumed mountain.

Panels with an intricate complexity of mechanized spiraling reds,
Igigi viewing leagues of stars from their perch,
Supreme orbiters of an endless track in the timeless glittering of the heavens,
Circling a bluish globe swirled with aqueous clouds nestled like a gem in the cosmos.
Lattice of vivid coloration reflected on a transparent domed helmet,
The orphan Zu planning a great rebellion to free the gods of their toil,
Seizing the crown of sovereignty with weapons of killing brightness
And fashioning a worker to bear the yoke,
Ninhursag's painless labor in the creation chamber of Eden.

Seer placing the Babylonian gem in a wrapping of black silk,
Meditating upon the panorama of time reflected in its polished depths:
A rebel who waged war with Enlil
That led to the creation of man,
Molded from the clay of earth and the blood of a slain god.
The rich florescence of civilization they hoped to extinguish with a deluge,
But for a boat on the teardrops of Enki
Who to his beloved sons sent a dove,
Sacred virgins bedecked in scarlet, harlots with goblets of starfire
And Magi who turn gold into bread, their wine spiced with exotic magic
Under skies radiating a fascination, which man will try to reach…
Magus in more mundane attire, passing women in mourning sable,
Grieving the burnoosed corpses of husbands
Who perished in a tempest of blinding sand
As an ancient relic is interred, Pazuzu, feared for evil plottings in the past.

Magistelli

A camel studded with gems of rivulets of sweat
Padding tirelessly over dunes and drifts,
Leaving footprints on the glittering crust.
Breath puffed as the platinum-rayed sun gleams, blinding the vast dust-dry horizon
Where no human souls wander 'neath the tranquil azure.
Astride the woven trappings, leaning closely to brass pommel,
A woman cloaked against the heat in a shimmer of color.
Pull aside that diaphanous gauze, O Favorite Daughter
With those shaded eyes green as absinthe,
Clinging to the lengthening purple shadows of the beast
While carried away to a place prepared in the desert of sand
Whose pitiless crimson wastes the coins have chosen
For a working of the wand.
For within this rider's soiled turban, bedecked with ornaments of violet,
Is nothing that is unworthy of the gods…

The oasis aflame in twilight, camel hobbled to a palm
Where the ring's jeweled fire fell on vellum.
Distant pyramids outlined in the dulling light of mauve,
With each drowsy eye-blink, O courtesan, rouse me from the borders of silken sleep,
Bringing rich Arabian diapasons, ether, and frictions of brandy
As thy enkindling spark.
The holy temple is opened under the infinite stars of night,
Its cubic altar purified with a brazen censer of fragrant smoke.
Olibanum, storax and myrrh rising in swirls and lazy curls,
Her perfumes burned 'neath the lamp of the moon.

Magus decorously clad in a fluttering abbai of scarlet,
Shaven, sunburned head shrouded by a nemyss of gold-trimmed black velvet.
Crouched in a circle of lit waxtapers dripping on a pentacle coated royal blue,
Meditating upon the starry vast, chanting incantations within the heart,
A lovesong of rapture devoted to the goddess
With the Operations of the Art soon at hand.

High Priestess shedding rays in a bespangled headdress,
Black hair plaited into braids with a gilded Uraeus coiled over her brows.
Averting those eyes rent asunder in antimony, for such painted beauty is a snare,
While rising from a robe of filmy indigo spread out as a carpet.
Her musky-sweet flesh white as ivory in the stifling darkness,
Afire with torques of amber, copper armlets, and the blaze of pendent agates.
Each lovely hand flashing finger-rings with bezels inlaid with scarabs,
The sun in the arms of khephra, coldly kissing the scepter of the realms.
Inspired magickal tool caressed by nails of opalescent lacquers
'Till the serpent, Hadit, bursts forth into flame.

Lioness playful on the tapestry of a sequined night,
Devoted true mistress girdled in jewels, postured lasciviously on a sandy bed.
In a dream of silver haze, lithe bodies yoked in sculptured embraces,
Bold lipstick smeared as the breath of mystical rapture is silenced with a kiss.
The fire-snake uncoils its splendor around an embryonic pearl,
Stone of magickal will transmuted in the furnace of ecstasy.
Dove bringing forth the wine of sunlight, poured into the glamour of the moon,
Paten and chalice of the Mass lifted to bright tiger teeth.
Stars perched over the burning desert as the sacrament is consumed,
Celebrants quaffing to the dregs ambrosial draughts of lunar gold.

Lying supine amongst the flame-patterns dancing all around,
Projecting thyself into the luster of night's star-gilt crown.
With the aura of a living talisman draw in the breath of thy gemmed rays,
Desiring earnestly the Child created from the fire of concentration.
Building up the visions with thy tongue's divine aroma,
Feasting on the vapors of the Graal's precious fruit.

Wax brilliant! O Lady of the forgotten gates
Whose key and seals are engraven with a burin in the rippling sand.
Invocations producing astral flecks of the goddess formulating,
Beauteous Queen in shimmering waves of night-blue tiffany
Rattling a sistrum of tambourine-bells.
In the limpid folds of her glorious stole the aspirant is draped,
Pressed to the bosom of Nuit to taste the galaxy's orange-gold milk.
With these withered sandals now in a pleasing orbit,
Blessed be the eyes that see the immortal mansions of Babalon,
Luxurious palace of the Cosmic Harlot anchored in the night.

A brazier of smoldering embers on a sparkling mound,
Resinous woods and gums lingering in the colors of sunrise
As shivering bodies awaken amid the saddle-bags.
Eyes behold with wonder the glazed stain of the sigil revealed
Where 'twas gently traced by finger on her royal flesh
From an amethyst bottle filled with the medicine of metals,
Dew of nourishing light from which the Magickal Child is fed.
Its secret enshrined in perfumed lampblack on illuminated pages,
Ingots aglitter for those who lift the peacock veil.
Literary treasures spread by poet and caravan from Baghdad to Spain
To the splendid Courts of Love.
Pull aside that diaphanous gauze, O Favorite Daughter
In whose garden blooms a flower of the rarest scent.
Look for it not by softly swaying palms in the shifting pageantry of a mirage,
But in the cooling shadows of lyricised moons.

Eroto-Comatose Lucidity

Kaleidoscopic lantern aglow in a thumbnail,
Magician on a cushioned divan with silken abbai unfastened.
Taken to the void of exhaustion by a vision of maddening glamour,
Luminous green eyes enchanted like absinthe.
Slippery nakedness in the flicker of pungent braziers,
Raven-tressed mistress of the prismatic moon.
Tool of flesh numbed from the erotic fire of lush red lips,
Repeated caresses of the chosen attendant.
Determined charms glistening with pearls of lustrous dew,
Hungering again to taste the breath of crimson.
Twitching muscles entangled in fragrant blue ribbons,
Smell of passion mingled with the spice of tarnished censers.
Sexual trance achieved by the dance of ecstasy,
Drowsy lids awakened at the gates of the kingdom of sleep.
Riding the exquisite wave of the pleasure spectrum,
Lightnings of bliss in the temple while approaching the borderland.
Heavy arousal though holding back the poison of the scepter,
Careful not to excite the spirits with tears of delight.
Visualizing the sigil with a deepward focus,
Desired object of the Working in the flash of a pendant.
Ravishing beauty engulfed by a river of darkness,
Scarlet paint of kisses on eyes heavily curtained…

Pillars of verd-antique in a nebulous haze,
Variegated sandiness stretching to horizons of infinite brilliance.
Opening eyelids aching for gorgeous revels,
Mouth scarlet and inviting 'neath the celestial cupola.
Naked in the dreamscape on an embroidered couch,
Lodge's mosaic floor covered with gusts of the dust of opals.
Vistas of a timeless realm betwixt the luxury of slumber,
Luster of a rosy face avidly seeking the alluring mask:
Jeweled scorpion amid the caravan of night,
Ornate hanging lantern in the frenzy of the harlot's emeralds,
Marvelous sunset while resting in the arms of Morpheus.

Nocturnal forays of an apparition in filmy draperies,
Dream-winged wraith gliding in cascades of amethyst.
Shimmering gown fallen away to reveal magnificent beauty,
Feminine gleams removed with her diaphanous sheath.
Statuesque figure brazen in the drifts of thuribles,
Delicacy of white curves nimbused against the glitter of stellar lamps.
Succubus attracted to the aura of the devotee,
Demanding a name from his magical lover in Le Desert Mauve.
Candidate embracing the projection of the shadow-woman
Adorned only with a pendant nestled at the throat.
Craving paradise in skin of exquisite, perfumed ivory,
Supple contours bathed in the stars' gilded rays.
Pallid, slender fingers held while raining a deluge of kisses,
Empurpled wand caressed with nails' iridescent lacquers.
True virginity silvered in patches of moonlight,
Saliva of the rose gemmed in soft honeyed hair.
Charging the resulting elixir while girded with lissome thighs,
Wisdom of bodies locked together with powerful spasms.
Cave of harmony receiving the polarity of the treasured jelly,
Raptures of sunbursts behind shuddering violet lids.
Ensigiled desire dissolved by flamelets of pleasure,
Womb of eternity pregnant with the envisioned gold.

Daath of Babalon

Arise!
Rocket of my child's eye gleaming in the arroyo sunrise,
Jewel-jetted scepter torn from the colors of pulps once marveled.
Roar, silver-tailed dragon whose living breath of death
Shakes the eternal lamps of night.
Lift my feet from the moss of earth to the glittering vault of space.
Trumpet my nativity under a bright witch-moon,
War-engine of the Aeon of Horus decked with banners of scarlet fire.
A garland to the righteous, a torment to the wicked
When seas of blood run from the crowned heads of scorpions,
Missile from the crucible of hell to storm the gates of heaven.

ENOCHIAN:

TORZU	*Arise!*
AAO IAL PIR GAH	*Amongst the flames of the first glory.*
YOR	*Roar!*
AVAVAGO GOHON	*For the thunders have spoken.*
GOHOLOR	*Lift up!*
VOHIM OL GIZ Y AZ	*With a hundred mighty earthquakes,*
ZONAC LUCIFTIAN	*Appareled with ornaments of brightness.*

BABALOND LOFOLO VEP ZOMD!
O Babalon, shineth as a flame
In the midst of your palace.
Burn!
Pearls of the flames of lust cast upon the chosen square,
Spirits in attendance, I destroy my treasure with the perfumes burnt.
Light a flame on an altar prepared with green and gold for the Working.
Arouse with wanton kisses she who charms the marrow of the wand.
Embrace with burning rapture in arabesques of sandal,
Renew the talisman that shines with the blood of birth,
Consecrate the sigil of devotion painted on a box of blackness.
Thee I evoke under the night-stars of the Mojave,
O Babalon, beloved, bring down your train of brightness,
Descend to triumph, a goddess enfleshed.

ENOCHIAN:

IALPON	*Burn!*
LIMLAL ZIEN	*Treasure of my own hand.*
OLPIRT IALPRT	*Light a flame*
SA TIANTA A BABALOND	*In the bed of a harlot*
DS ABRAMG	*Which I have prepared*
BUS DIR TILB VNIGLAG	*So that the glory of her descends*
CAOSG	*Upon the earth.*

BABALOND LOHOLO VEP ZOMD
O Babalon, shineth as a flame
In the midst of your palace.
Arise!
The dark rites now concluded, Babalon I await your secret sign,
Appear with the dawn of the One mightier than all the kings of earth,
Magical child of the elemental who answered my summons,
Supreme spell of love-feasts in the infernal chapel,
In my hooded radiance, perfect consummate union of sorcery and science.
Now a wanderer in the abyss, drunk on the gilded cup of madness,
My star fallen as the hour strikes, flame of the crystal prophecy.
Free from the lying hypocrisy, I conquer both death and hell,
Taken to the stars on wings I had only known in dreams.
Let the truth be known to the least of men, each an embryo god.

ENOCHIAN:

TORZU	*Arise!*
AAO HUBARDO TIBBP	*Amongst the lanterns of sorrow.*
TZAMRAN	*Appear (in nine moons)*
AAF NOR MOLAP	*Amongst the sons of men*
IZIPOP	*From the highest vessels,*
FOARGT VRAN	*The dwelling place of the elders*
LUCIFTIAS PIRIPSOL	*In the brightness of the heavens.*

Blue Lipstick

Hot vermilions and lacy opalescents,
Techniques of disguise in the sorcery of tropical foliation.
Stifling, luxurious flora dripping rain-prisms on verdure-robed underwood.
Pigments of lizards on vines shrouded in gemmed mists
Coiled languidly amid the tapestry of burgeoning, exotic plantlets.
Eidolon of a sparkling paradise descending from the kala's black majesty.
Inner eyelids jeweled with birds scattering
From the shining veil. Wings of silver-gold dragon
Unfolding to reflect cascades of moist, iridescent ferns.
Primordial heart-beat advancing in the avalanche of lush exudations,
Gaining proximity attracted to the aura of the dreaming mirror:
Sun-bronzed anatomy enthroned on a silken rainbow,
Inhaling the cloying scent of variegated orchid-buds,
Projections of her magical sleep while receiving the stellar influx.
Ecstasies of the priestess trafficking with those betwixt,
Protected from the hypnotic mask of the royal seraphim
During the climax tinged with the vivid bouquet of scarlet.
Paint of sapphire repelling the trance of terror,
Flame-colored reptilian pupils ignited by the smell of crimson.
Beatitude of metallic gleams dulling in rank, decomposing vegetation,
Fighting the urge to shape-shift amid the expelled treasure of red.
Dank, noxious aromas of a morass draped with magenta lianas,
Impassioned breathing of the generator of images,
Bare coppery feet joyful in the rubied mud.

Lachrymatory

Pale emerald moon upon the catafalque of engilded Qa'a,
Prismatic scorpion in crackling torchlight.
Flame-rayed mummy in a royal sarcophagus with painted vignettes,
Funerary jackals in black and gold and dull glowing crimson,
Spectral pageant of ancient Khem.
Brown-serpentine swathe cut with tools of the mortuary craft,
Turquoise bottle to gather the gemmed tears of the Pharaoh.
Delicate incrustation of a trepanned cranium,
Purple gloves of Hotepsekheumi holding the treasure of sepia,
Serpent-hooded gleams and the pelts of magenta zebra.
Lords of Amenta lifting the opal veil of a beetle-black sun,
Cadaverous phantasms of a harlequin charioteer,
Stars a-glitter in night blue over crocodile of river mud.

Commentary

These lachrymals or lachrymatories were small vases, urns, or vials that have been found in ancient Roman sepulchers and were believed by latter-day historians to have been receptacles which contained the tears of mourners. However, it is only a modern-day conjecture that these narrow-necked, tear-shaped bottles were placed in tombs according to an ancient custom of putting the tears of the deceased person's surviving relatives and friends in them as memorials of affection and sorrow as it is very difficult to find any trace of such a custom in ancient writings. According to at least one student of esoteric Atlanteanology, the Romans believed these tears had special powers, and many of these lachrymal urns contained representations of a single eye on them. Often found in tomb reliefs from ancient Egypt, this was the divine eye or egg of the sacred pregnancy whose true meaning continues to elude both Egyptological scholarship and most genuine seekers of hidden knowledge. On some reliefs, the teardrops shed by the divine eye are shown turning into wings.

Reliquary

Manduca panem tuum cum silentio

Beauseant

Neglected gloom of a castle bathed in pale brilliance,
Gaunt stone parapets like fingers pointing starkly at the moon.
Semi-circle of lanterns aglow on the crumbling flagstones,
Dim, yellow cast upon weather-bleached, mortared walls.
Dark-robed figures seated in a pentagon traced on the shadowy courtyard,
Members of a fraternal Order participating in a séance
With the medium contacting the spirits of the ancient Lords.
Templar ruin perched on a hilltop above a craggy gorge in the Pyrenees,
Traces of ramparts as vestiges of its blood-soaked past.
Vague glints in damp mist rising from slopes of broom,
Witnessing an apparition materializing at the stroke of midnight.
Specter of a helmeted rider in quilted armor upon his traveling mount,
Purity of white mantle emblazoned with a red cross pattee.
Conjured warrior-monk upon a dappled gray steed,
Templar of Bezu keeping ghostly vigil among pine and eucalyptus.
Bridle jingling while approaching the nocturnal gathering
Through the archway of the fortified priory,
Dilapidated mossy remains of a cullised gateway.
Raiment of whiteness glittering with heraldic crimson thread,
Shield devoid of ornamentation and an austere hilted sword.
Removing a mail-helmet of gleaming silver before the high initiates,
Revealing the bearded face of a monastic knight with tousled hair
Mounted on armored war-horse with a chequered banneret,
Black and white flutter against the star-bright night.
Lineaments of the phantom knight with an ectoplasmic aura,
Uttering an evocative message from the world of spirit.
Conveying to the medium the true natures of the Order,
Encoded within the colorful tapestry of myth and legend.

Mfkzt

Elegant silhouettes of noble birthright,
Resplendent tapers reflected in the gleam of the banqueting hall.
Glasses of aromatic balsams censing the pageantry of the Graal feast,
Rubies and sapphires, dragons and doves.
Rare carpets in the lighted hall of a hilltop citadel
Bedecked with pillars of malachite topped with gilded capitals.
Walls draped with silk hangings and flashing banners of azure,
Blue taffeta curtain with arcana in harlequin.
Valorous knights in the effulgence of twinkling candelabra,
Seated before a sumptuous table in the firewood's scent.
High-born damsels on gemmed ivory stools,
Zodiacal jewels sewn into the rich furnishings.
Maidens in red samite with capes of ermine,
Decorously gowned in gloriously colorful ciclatoun and sendel.
Tranquil amber glow of rich, twisted beeswax,
Prismatic goblets of chased moonsilver
Radiant in the dazzling lights like breastplates of fire;
Dedicated seekers initiated into a sublime mystery.
Ornate vestures of the majestic spectacle,
Hermetic regalia and phoenix wand.
Flame-patterns of dark orange jacinth in a jewel-encrusted scepter,
King's lustrous fabric trimmed in purple velvet.
Richly-embroidered pentalpha on an emerald green tablecloth,
Jeweled reliquary of gold containing an embalmed head.
Skin of Egyptian copper touched only with violet gloves,
Lineage of extreme antiquity with unblemished, mysterious features.
Iridescent blade of a decorated tailleoir,
Sparkling eyes of a chthonic specter in the aureole of eastern candles.
Grains of paradise burning in gilt thuribles,
Ciborium with the iridized metallic bread of angels.
Riches of glittering veins mined in the ritually-incised cranium,
Paradise stone ground into the powder of a white rainbow.
Elegant dust of death blown through an ornate straw
To those questers receiving visions from the Templar kiss:
Ingesting royalty with the feast of highward metals,
Skeletal platinum consumed by the owls of eternity.

Jynx

Camel bells dulling in a magenta sky,
Thieves in a gloomy labyrinth choking on the perfume of death.
Crackling torch revealing jackals flanking a gilded tomb,
Mummy casing embellished with a painted tableau.
Shroud of linen in the orange flicker,
Severed mummified head removed from a bespangled sarcophagus.
Unearthed grisly relic containing a lustrous black unguent,
Residue of pineal activity secreted by enlightened beings.
Golden Tear of the Eye of Horus in the tissue's exquisite decay,
Occultum of harlequin entombed in the royal necropolis.
Spoils of diademed serpents in granite coffers,
Prized ouroboric mummia sealed in jars of alabaster.
Sepulchral honey prepared into conical bread-cakes,
Spiced white loaves consumed in the sanctuary of Thoth.
Infernal sacrament of the Djedhi priesthood,
Feeding the rainbow body with the glitter of the sleepers.
Sight of the blue pearl in the shining crown,
Projected by black crystal obelisks beyond the veil of illusion.
Focusing the light-body into the region of Duat,
Isis enthroned in a flame of amethyst.
Pillared temple of variegated marble,
Sisterhood of serpents with hair fantastically dressed.
Sacred priestesses draped in black gauze
With tiaras of gold like frozen celestial rays.
Virgins of the imperial court pouring forth scarlet nectar,
Noble rivulets of milk laced with holy starfire.
Kingly recipients receiving sustenance from the divine menstruum,
Solidified light from the prism of the moon enfleshed.
Sacred chalice at the monthly feast,
Precious treasured blood ladled in a gemmed dipper.
Endocrinal hormones of a greater saturation,
Immortal liquor of the dark Nile's dragon kingship.
Kings in vermilion anointed with the jeweled wine of crocodiles,
Masters of shaping, charmers of making.
Broidery of splendor ships against the starry plains,
Atlantean kings of opalescent turquoise waters.

Tailleoir

Distinctive red cross on a glittering white surcoat,
Phantom rider with the gleam of moonlit silver armor.
Misty shapes of ancient ruins in the candle glow,
Ectoplasmic profile of the Templar vanishing with a milky luminescence.
Séance concluded with its visions of the Gnostic Mass,
Hallows of the royal feast in the radiance of molten beeswax.
Bronze-flecked ringlets of rosy figures draped in lordly silk,
Painted daubs of maidens in the company of the Graal.
Mysterious object of illumined knight-mystics,
Sworn guardians of a head kept in a filigreed casket.
Depository of treasure in lichen-enshrouded grottoes,
Pecuniam infinitam amid the phosphorus of slumber.
Hushed whispers of secret elitism,
Confessions of medieval heretics in flickering dungeons:
Supremely abominable rites in the hell-glow of midnight ceremonies,
Trampling on the crucifix and blaspheming the Father's name.
Idolatry with the gilded bone of a ritually-trepanned skull,
Dark utterances from the brazen lips of an oracle.
Unimagined revelations from the Supreme Initiatrix,
Black Virgin with a multicolored halo in a subterranean crypt;
Possessors of the jeweled fire of the serpents of wisdom.
Encoding the alchemical opus with sculptured designs,
Murmur of Latin stained with gemmed light,
Intricate stone weaves of cathedrals flamboyantly Gothic.
Emblematic regalia of the knights of Ordo Draconis,
Steel of damascened claymore with ivory pommel.
Passwords of a submerged cult to their Masonic brethren,
Protectors of a royal lineage, Le Serpent Rouge.

The Black Wine of Owls

Gleam of silver chalice in the lights of the Mass,
Monks in dark-cowled robes seated at the opulence of the table.
Uncorked aroma breathing in the candle's amber radiance,
Wine of Sangraal fermented in the sanctified vessel.
Vintage of divine kings harvested in small yields,
Extracting richness in pressings of glorious fruition,
Bleeding the jeweled grapes of the promised land.
Fragrance of the colors of sunlight in a fertile valley,
Templar sanctuary in the prism of green vineyards.
Noble purple clusters of the treasured dirt of Khem,
Rarest elements in the fecund brilliance of the earth.
(lapis lappus exillis stellis)
Marvelous properties of ore with the bloom of ripeness,
Celestial fire of ******* absorbed in the roots.
Lifting the veil with each quaff of the luscious bursting,
Harlequin dreams of the arcana of liberating.
Voyage in the kaleidoscope in a moment of apocalypse,
Beatific visions beyond the trance of sorrow.
Tincture of sapphire in veins of the precious blood of royalty,
Graal-kings drunk with gilded starry wisdom.
Transmuting the human with the alchemist's quintessence,
Dregs of blessing consumed in gem-encrusted hallows.
Heirs to eternity with a mutation of cobalt,
Shedding monastic vestments for the rainbow pallium.
Riders of a winged horse against night's magic pallet,
Through the arched gateways into the tapestry of heaven.
Ancient initiated wisdom encoded in decorated stone,
Secret process of viticulture bordered by gargoyles at twilight.
Blue apples of gnosis reserved for the diadem of the elite,
To drink like a Templar in the aura of shining angels.
Elixir of jeweled grapes from cherished black soil,
Serpent of paradise in the majesty of a silver chalice.

Ophiuchus

Dusky ivory concubine in the pleasure tent,
Azure of oriental perfumes coiled about the extremities of bliss.
Nakedness upon gilded pillows covered with sapphires,
Germ of wheels of flaming scarlet 'neath the peacock crown.
Raptures offering the wine of a burning rainbow,
Vistas of paradise unfolding to eyes enslaved by fantastic tricks.
Variegated desert tread with amethyst sandals,
Opalescent scarab of the moon flashing in the illuminated deeps.
Seven-headed serpent wearing the diadem of midnight,
Purity of magician banishing the glamours of luminous venom.
Ceaseless weaving of pageantry from the exoteric sun,
Caravan of dreams laden with the tapestry of earthly treasures.
Child devoured by Saturn ensnared in a glittering web,
Ebony skeleton dancing upon its flowery tomb.
Gemmed green flame beaconing the dove of twilight,
Fire of revelation glimpsed from the infinite unmanifest.

Scorpion's refulgent glory, Archer's sparkling missile,
Serpent-Bearer opening the secret gateway;
Guiding the pilgrim to sanctuary in the stellar labyrinth,
Void of shining darkness beyond the sevenfold veil.

Green falcon alighting upon the heart of the aurora,
Slayer of the fleece of the iridescent lamb with seven eyes.
Eighth chakra opened in the trance of beatitude,
Spectrum of illusions dissolved in the garden of mystery.
Prince drinking the colors of Isis in the aura of the honey-vessel.
Bedecked in the purple robe of mystical kingship.
Sacred island of jewels reached with Luzifer's recovered wings,
Silver plumage of swan gliding across the starry drapery.
Midnight angels trumpeting at the palace of gleaming pillars,
Fields of Arcadia blossoming in the sun's black majesty.
Aurific seed hidden in the womb of eternity,
Beyond the prism of light in the portal of the snake-nebula.
Lotus-flower of Da'ath in waters of harlequin fish,
Facets of the crown adorning the daughter of the violet star.
Ray of esoteric luminary shining upon the king of radiant blood
Enthroned in etheric blue with a nimbus of immortality.

Calix Horroris*

Violet eyes shine.
Jeweled water of the living grail,
Gilded, stainless vessel 'neath the prismatic lamp of Abraxas.
Night-blue draperies a-glitter with cosmic opulence,
Tides of blood aurified in her sacred chalice.
Radiant white-plumed dove shedding tears of rainbow wine,
Mooncup of red-gold with swirls of oily iridescence.
Lady of the serpent holding a richly-crowned babe,
Nurtured with gemmed drops of the milk of paradise.
Face enhaloed with light, adored by amethyst-lidded eyes,
Child of great serenity protected by majestic wings,
Perfumed gauze of the vesture of the dragon-queen,
Spooned from a magical bowl the rich food† of the matrix,
Extracts of the perfect ruby flowing from her hidden spring,
Bestowing mystic sight to the prince in wisps of azure garment,
A wondrous flowering upon the deathless green.

---

* Many students of Crowleyan sex-magick will no doubt interpret this verse to be associated with a specific ritual that involves Tantric fluids known as the *Elixir Rubeus*. However, even with the line "Extracts of the perfect ruby flowing from her hidden spring", this is not the case. Here, the living grail of the deathless green contains "tears of prismatic fire collected in an engilded tomb." Therefore the blood in the *Calix Horroris* (Cup of Horror) comes from the 'Heart of the Deeps', which is the true hidden spring, and that which facilitates the Grand Dreaming of a Treasured Eye.

† Among the Court Cards (Minor Arcana) of the "Thoth" tarot deck, the 'Knight of Disks' (Fire of Earth) is unique in many ways to the other (brother) knights. Although Crowley states that the function of this particular card "is entirely confined to the production of food", it is the highly esoteric nature of the harvest from these fertile lands and cultivated fields that should be meditated upon (but, again, not in deceptive moonlight). This 'ripe corn from the soil' is more clearly revealed, perhaps, by the corresponding King of Diamonds in a regular card deck – a harlequin who speaks in a black tongue indeed.

www.ingramcontent.com/pod-product-compliance
Lightning Source LLC
Chambersburg PA
CBHW030941150426
42812CB00064B/3089/J